Single to Triple Figures Per Hour

Single to Triple Figures
Per Hour

HOW A BATHER KICKSTARTED THEIR SOLO-GROOMER DOG SPA

Betty Peto

Single to Triple Figures Per Hour: How a Bather Kickstarted Their Solo-groomer Dog Spa

FIRST EDITION

This book contains advice and information relating to dog grooming and business management. It is intended to be a supplemental aid. All efforts have been made to ensure the accuracy of this book's information as of the publication date.

ISBN 978-1-7340203-0-4 (hc)

ISBN 978-1-7340203-1-1 (pb)

ISBN 978-1-7340203-4-2 (ebook)

Ordering Information: ingramspark.com or contact the author: betty@wholesomegroomingacademy.com

Credits

Author: Peto, Betty

Front Cover Image: © Tatyana Kalmatsuy / Adobe Stock

Back Cover Image: © mdorottya / Adobe Stock

Cover Design: Uvarov, Mykhailo

Developmental editing and proofreading: Slagle, Stephanie www.stephanieslagle.com

Developmental editing: Levi, Peto

Interior Design: Spears, Brent www.brentspears.com

Subjects: Business Positioning - Dog Grooming - Gentle Dog Handling - Compassionate Dog Training - Compassionate Dog Grooming.

This book is dedicated to those who want to thrive physically, mentally, and financially as a groomer.

Create the work-life balance that you desire!
Your destiny is in your hands.

And I am here to help you.

Introduction

Hi, I'm Betty. Nice to meet you! Are you thinking about becoming a groomer but worried about the transition and how it will play out? Do you feel overwhelmed and confused about which steps to take in what order?

Let me share how I did it as encouragement to help you break out of the rat race and become your own boss in style.

Note that I did it from scratch, with very little money to juggle, zero marketing skills, and very limited grooming experience, with English as my second language, starting out at the wise age of twenty-five, in 2013.

This book is part 1 of a series. It focuses on explaining how I went from being a bather at a salon to owning my own dog spa and how I scaled my business and managed to charge triple figures per hour for grooming dogs.

Part 2 of the series will teach you how to implement the skills I gained over the years to start and grow your business even faster than I did.

Chapter 1

The Beginning:
How I Became a Groomer

I've always loved animals and had cats and dogs throughout my child-hood. I dreamed about becoming a veterinarian as a kid. I had the desire to heal animals, the curiosity for science, the love of animals, and the stomach for the profession, but I didn't have the brains or the heart to deal with a steady flow of ignorant or abusive clients on a regular basis. Being on call was not too appealing either, given I love to sleep.

In my first year of college, I volunteered at a dog shelter to overcome my fear of dogs, which stemmed from a childhood incident. When I was about eleven years old, I was running to meet a friend a few streets down from our house when a pack of stray dogs encircled me at the edge of our town. Luckily, my dad heard me screaming, so he came running and got me out of there just as the dogs started nipping my pants by my ankle. I developed PTSD over this experience. My body would become drenched in sweat every single time I saw a loose dog on the street. I loved dogs nevertheless, so I wanted to overcome this fear and understand when they wanted to bite and why, so I could change their mind and avoid getting bitten.

That's how I ended up at the shelter in my late teen years when I started college. I got an award from the city for my help at the shelter. They gave out the awards at the city's annual ceremony and they had the local dog school perform there. I was in awe about the dogs' skills, and I went to volunteer at the dog training school to learn more about their magic tricks. I liked it a lot, so much so that I became a dog trainer. It seemed to be a good match. I started leading and assisting in group classes in my mother tongue at the dog school, and also gave private lessons at peoples' home in my mother tongue and English. I rented a room in an apartment with other college students to make ends meet, but I wanted to have my own place where I could have my own dogs.

One day as I was heading home to my parents, who lived in a tiny town in the south, I met a fascinating woman, Andi, on the train. She was talking about her job in England. She was so passionate about it and explained how easy it was to make good money there. She passed around paper pounds for us to see in the cabin, so we could get a feel of the foreign currency, and I was hooked. I asked her to exchange numbers because I had to get off the train shortly and catch another one, but I wanted to talk to her about this some more. I messaged her and we talked and talked for days. Flames of passion burst to life inside of me, and I made a decision.

I put my training career on hold for a bit and I moved to England within a month of meeting Andi on the train. My goal was to earn enough money as a live-in caregiver to the elderly to kickstart my life and buy my first house.

My mom was furious about me dropping out of college and going abroad alone, but I was beyond dedicated. Little did she know, not long after this I would be flying even farther away than England.

I arrived safely at the company in Salisbury I'd gotten hired at and started working for my first client within a few days.

I read Cesar Millan's first book, Cesar's Way, in my free time between job duties and I wanted to meet him. I got a ticket and went to his show at the Wembley Stadium in London in 2010, and after that I wanted to work for him. Every single person I told about my dream laughed at me or called me straight up crazy. I was stubborn enough to not care, and I put everything on the red and bought a ticket to Los Angeles.

I needed info about cheap hotels and food, so I was digging on IWIW (a type of Hungarian social media back then) for people who lived in Los Angeles and spoke Hungarian. That was my passionate attempt to connect with people from my country who were already living in Los Angeles for advice. I was digging through years of data and found two random but promising persons, Agi and Levi, who were giving kind and caring advices to others. I read their comments from almost two years back to other people on different topics, and they seemed to be real humans and reliable to talk to.

I messaged them both about my plan to go to LA, and Agi was super helpful. We were chatting and after she learned about me buying my flight ticket, she offered a free room in her house and to pick me up from the airport after I landed. I was incredibly grateful for her beyond generous offers.

Levi was helpful as well, but he didn't seem to believe I'd really come to the US. As it turned out later, he tried to help many people with info on how to make it in the US who messaged him on IWIW before me, but none of them made it to the US, so he didn't want to waste his time on another "wannabe." It came across in his letters, so I didn't push it. I'd already gotten an in with Agi, so I brushed it off by saying "you will see" in my head. I thanked him for his help so far and left it at that.

The day came when I went to the Heathrow Airport in London with my luggage. I was ready for the huge adventure. As I put my passport on the check-in counter, I was informed that my flight had been canceled due to the Eyjafjallajökull volcano erupting in Iceland. My flight was the first one that got canceled. Bummer. Biiig bummer. It was quite a setback, but nothing could stop me at this point. I was ready to hitch-hike on a ship to get to the US. After ten days of waiting in London and couch surfing at friends' houses, my flight finally got to depart and I was on my way to California.

My mom was a nervous wreck about my trip. She was sure Agi was a 300-pound man and I'd be sold as a prostitute or portioned out as an unwilling organ donor. I understood there was a chance of that, but my dedication and gut powered through the worry and I saw it as an incredible opportunity.

I messaged Agi when I landed, and she picked me up right away. She was a girl, just as I had hoped for, and everything she said turned out to be true.

She let me stay in her house for a while and it was a lifesaver.

I rented the cheapest car available at the rental and went to the address I found on Google for Cesar's Dog Psychology Center. The car rental company printed a paper map for me because the GPS was not working in the car. I didn't have the chops to negotiate for a car that had working GPS, so I rolled with it.

I finally arrived at the place and it was there, just as I had hoped for. I had my little letter in my hand and I told the guy at the gate my name and that I wanted to meet with Cesar and I would be the happiest person on Earth if I could volunteer here and pick up dog poop at the facility. I literally said all of this. He told me this was a private property and I had to leave right now or he'd call the cops.

I asked if I could leave my letter there for Cesar before I left. He took it and I went to the car. I parked a few streets down because I could not see a thing on the road through the tears pouring down my face. I'd traveled 10,000 miles, I'd found the place, but I couldn't get past the freaking gate.

After I calmed down, I drove the rental car back and started working on my next plan to get in. I told myself I'd come this far, I wasn't going to give up just yet.

I posted a photo on social media as a sign of life for my friends that I was alive and sipping Starbucks under palm trees in the sun. It was a nice change from the cloudy, cold, and rainy weather I'd withstood for the sake of my dream in England. Levi saw the image and hit me up, asking about those palm trees. He suspected I was not in London anymore. I told him yes indeed, I was in the US. We chatted and he asked me whether I had seen the ocean yet. Agi lived in the valley and I hadn't been able to go to the beach yet, so he offered to take me. I asked Agi and she somewhat knew Levi via a friend and she told me he was safe to be around. I was ready to see the ocean. Levi showed up on the weekend to take me to the beach.

In Europe you get used to guys ogling you, whistling around you, making comments all the time. I was shocked by Levi not showing any signs of interest, given his European heritage. His no-reaction behavior was surprising enough for me that at first I thought he was gay. Later he told me he liked me a lot, but he didn't want to be pushy at all, just wanted to help me get to see the ocean.

He took me to the Dog Beach in Huntington Beach and we visited Laguna Beach right after. Both places were breathtaking to me. We grabbed a bite at a local restaurant and he took me back to Agi's. We talked and talked after this, and I liked him a lot but was still not sure which team he was playing for.

We kept chatting for a couple of days, and he finally started to open up. He told me he played guitar and I asked him to play me something sometime. He agreed. So, we met up again.

We were an instant click from then on. We hit it off and he asked me to move in after like three dates. Everybody warned me not to do it. I didn't listen and I'm so glad. We are celebrating our 10th wedding anniversary this year. Turns out he is just as crazy as I am, in a good way.

We spent three months together in Huntington Beach, CA. I had to go back to Europe due to my visa expiring, but he invited me back for another three months.

I could not wait to come back. Not long after I arrived, we went to a Barnes & Noble to get Cesar's newest book. Levi saw a poster that said Cesar was coming to Huntington Beach to do a book signing in a few days. Needless to say, I was jumping out of my skin. I prepared my little three-sentence speech, practiced it for days, and went to the store like two hours early the day of to make sure I wouldn't miss Cesar. To my shock, there was already a line, like 15–20 people in front of me. I was wearing my "Dog whisperer" T-shirt and baseball cap for the occasion that I'd gotten at his show in London. That was a nice icebreaker when it was my turn in front of him. I will never forget, he asked: "Did you get that in Australia?" I took a deep breath and I said with a trembling voice and a strong Hungarian-British accent, "No, in London. I saw your lovely show, traveled 10,000 miles twice to see you and I would be the happiest person on Earth if I could see the Dog Psychology Center. Would you please let me see it?" I was so nervous I almost cried at this point, not believing I was talking to HIM. He smiled and said, "Sure." My jaw dropped. So did the others behind me.

While I was gasping for air out of disbelief and joy, he was signing my books I'd brought and he told his assistant to hook me up with the center's director, Adriana, to arrange a visit for me at the center. I could not believe it.

The same guy, Jose, who'd told me to go away a few months ago let me in this time around and drove me around the property on a quad with the kindest demeanor, answering all my silly questions with the greatest patience. I asked him and Adriana to sign a book that Cesar had signed as a memento of meeting them. Adriana gave me T-shirts signed by Cesar for Levi and me as a gift. It was amazing.

I met a dozen more times with Adriana, Blizzard, and Junior (dogs from Cesar's puppy book) while I was in the US. It was a long drive from HB, but it was so worth it.

During this second visit, I befriended Levi's ex-wife, Edit (I know, it's weird, but we are good friends to date.), and I explained my dilemma to her. I realized dog training involves teaching people more than teaching dogs. Dogs picked up my signals way faster than people learned to undo their old habits, which were the main causes of dogs "misbehaving." I realized I desired a "less work with people and more work with dogs" job. I even had a fridge magnet: "The more people I meet, the more I love my dogs."

She raised the question, why didn't I become a groomer? I was like, I am a countryside girl and there is no way that I'd do nail painting and hair dying. Those (along with other grooming services) are not aligned with my pet care philosophy; neither are wanted nor enjoyed by dogs, in my opinion. Then she calmly explained to me how big the market was for groomers and that I didn't have to do those things if I didn't want to. She opened my eyes that there was space for a "natural groomer" in the industry. Boy, was she right!

She said I could combine my training experience with grooming and offer more of a wholesome way of grooming dogs. Like creating a "one doggy at a time" business profile and providing more of an exclusive service. I gave it a thought and the idea deeply resonated with me in this light. So, I decided to switch careers and become a groomer.

Adriana invited me to their Christmas Party. My visa expired about a week before the party, so I had to go back to Europe. I applied for a student visa to make it back on time to the party, but it got denied and I couldn't come back to the US. I was heartbroken.

After the initial disappointment of the visa denial, Levi and I started talking about our relationship. We both liked each other a lot and wanted to figure out how could we convert this long-distance relationship into living together. He proposed to me not long after on one of his visits on a ship restaurant on the Danube. He said the kindest things and then asked me to marry him. I was ready to say yes long ago, but finally I could say it. He flew to see me every 3–6 months in Europe while we waited for the approval of my fiancée visa. It was beyond tough, but I knew what I was waiting for, so making it through was never a question. I just couldn't wait to get to him.

Levi helped me see the opportunity of studying to become a groomer while I waited back in Europe. I had the honor of taking care of his mom in her last years until she died in 2012. My live-in caregiver experience came in very handy and brought great comfort to her in her final months.

When I finally returned to the US after 19 months of hellish waiting, we got married barefoot in the sand in Newport Beach, CA. It was the best day of my life. Funny enough that we picked that gorgeous beach not because it was the fanciest one around, but because weirdly enough it had the rule that you could get married there without a permit, first come, first served.

Adriana was no longer a part of the team at the center by the time I came back, so that opportunity kind of vanished for me. I was sad, but still dedicated and had high hopes for myself. My training methods had changed a lot and Cesar's methods didn't seem that appealing to me anymore. I'd learned about more "working with" instead of "doing to" methods to collaborate with dogs. It was more fun for me (and for the dogs) to train them with more creativity and attention that kept them engaged. I felt in peace with the new direction I was taking.

I had my grooming certificate, but given my lack of work experience at grooming salons, I took a bather position to get me started on the corporate ladder.

It helped me get a closer view of how a large facility works in the US and also helped me raise more questions about the profession, allowing me to fine-tune the way I preferred to work.

I didn't like the rush, the crazy number of dogs we had to work on per day, the dogs' anxiety, the cages, the horribly short lunch breaks (if we got any at all), and the way dogs were treated and handled in general. It was like a factory, manufacturing "clean dogs" from "dirty ones" with haircuts often not aligned with the dog's actual needs. They were solely focusing on profit and exploiting employees and dogs.

A few weeks in, I either started or finished my shifts crying at home or in the car, and I knew that I could not participate in this kind of service anymore.

I imagined a radically different experience for dogs and groomers alike, so when Levi's job relocated us from California to Texas, I was relieved and we started talking about how we could make it happen.

Chapter 2

Starting My Own Business

Choosing a Grooming Business Setup

I dreamed about owning my own salon (it sounded so fancy), but I didn't have the balls at first to go through with it. I kind of thought I'd used up all my luck for now and I didn't want to challenge my faith any further. So, I was thinking about taking the "safe and comfortable" route and getting a job at Wendy's, and whenever I had the funds to do the salon, I would jump in and get it going.

Levi saw that I was entertaining the idea of opening a salon, but I needed a little clarity and a push to make it happen. So he told me, what if we jumped in right now? I was happy that he encouraged me to give it a try, but I was pretty surprised that he believed in me so much that he was willing to help fund my new career. Levi told me that I could pay him back whenever I made enough profit. It was just the push I needed. We agreed that he'd help me buy the essential tools to get started, I would give it my all, we'd hope for the best, and we'd see how it went.

I started thinking about what kind of business setup I wanted to work in.

At the groomer school, they hadn't taught us much about opening our own shop, only how to work for someone else. Levi told me to research what kind of options were out there.

After some digging, I found a few exciting alternatives to consider.

Grooming Setup Options

- **Having your own salon** (renting or buying a retail shop)
- **Mobile groomer** (buying a grooming van)
- **House call groomer** (using your car and grooming dogs at the client's house)
- **Becoming an employee at a salon** (you are employed or rent a table at someone else's salon)
- **Grooming salon in your home** (setting up a dog spa at home)

I wanted to make this decision very carefully to make sure I wouldn't regret anything and I wouldn't get stuck in a vortex of an unfitting choice and end up in an "I have to stick it out or go bankrupt" situation.

That is the kind of situation many new groomers get into when big pet supply companies (that also offer grooming services on site) lure them into grooming training by paying for their tuition. New groomers get stuck with the company and the horrible work situation for years unless they pay back the price of training and the penalty fee.

So, to avoid a similar situation, I listed out my feelings, my needs and preferences, and the pros and cons of each option.

My Feelings

When I thought about setting up my own salon, I felt:

- Excited
- Worried
- Hopeful

- Overwhelmed
- Passionate
- Dedicated

My Needs & Preferences

- **Financial stability** – Creating a trustworthy cash flow fast enough without a huge loan burden and setting my own prices.
- **Comfort** – Setting my own rules and business hours, no over-whelming shifts or early or super late starts/finishes. Eating by the table, on a comfy chair, hair free. (Well mostly, haha, but definitely not by the grooming table standing or in the storage room sitting on a box of supplies, how I used to eat lunch at work.)
- **Peace** – Working on only a small number of dogs per day, with no rush to get through each one. A business setup that's easy to back out of in case something doesn't work out, or I get sick, or something else comes up.
- **Freedom** – To choose the workflow and customize canine care on my own, to set my own pace.
- **Closeness** – Spending the most time possible with my family as quality time (avoiding "layover times" by driving in traffic.)
- **Joy** – Being there for my husband and pets to enjoy their company and witness their milestones in life.
- **Ease** – Having time to cook a healthy lunch during my lunch break and eat at noon.
- **Health** – Using only non-toxic products and having tools and tables customized to my height to care for my back.
- **Excellence** – Taking my time and prioritizing quality over quantity.
- **Flexibility** – Spending more time on a dog if needed (shy or anxious dogs).

These needs and preferences roughly covered what I was looking for, so Levi and I put the options under the microscope.

Mobile Groomer Option

I thought about becoming a mobile groomer first since it provides a pretty chill environment for doggies, and I could charge higher rates. But I didn't like the idea of making a significant investment in a van and driving that much daily. Levi brought up some of the other cons.

He asked me, "Do you want to get cooked in a box in the Texan heat? Or shiver on the cold winter days? Or listen to a loud AC above your head all day? Do you want to deal with all the humidity and loose dog hair circulating in there? Do you want to drive from client to client in this crazy traffic? Where will you go to the bathroom? Where will you eat lunch? Is that the quality of life you want, eight hours a day, five days a week? We'll need to invest a lot in a van, and what if you hate it two weeks in?"

It hit me hard that this was not the quality of life I wanted. The mobile groomer option was out the window for me at that instant.

Retail Salon Rent/Buy

I didn't like the idea of all the responsibility that comes with renting a retail shop, like hiring people and all the investment and commitments I would need up front. Renting a retail shop has a longer base lease time than renting a house. It was a 2–5 year contract for a location. So, I would've had to stick it out for several years even if the place was not as profitable as we had hoped for, or break the contract and lose significant money. So, we dug further.

Renting a table at an existing salon could have been a cheaper option, but I didn't find it appealing. I felt my philosophy wouldn't fit in the usual type of salon atmosphere. The way I wanted to groom dogs was so unique; I wouldn't have been able to do the peaceful setup (working one-on-one with dogs) there—due to too much distraction.

Owning a retail shop was an option as well. Though you don't "throw money out" like when you're renting, it seemed a huge risk, and the commitments this option came with were not aligned with the profit increase that we predicted.

We did the math, and with the significantly higher expenses of owning a salon, employing many people, it would leave us with only a 10–20 percent increase in profit. Plus loads of investing not to compromise quality, give decent salaries to employees, and not exploit doggy clients. We concluded that leasing and owning a salon was out of the question for now due to financial reasons and us being beginners.

Becoming an Employee

I like my independence a lot, writing my own rules as much as possible, and being my own boss. So, I took a long, hard look at working for someone else and getting sucked into the corporate world of grooming. At this point, my gut screamed at me to be brave, go for it, and make it work on my own.

Being an employee was out of the idea basket for me as well.

House Call Groomer or Working from Home

The final options were to become a house call groomer or set up my salon at home. We were leaning toward the working from home option as the best solution for us. Once again, we listed the pros and cons.

Pros of Working from Home

- No extra lease
- I could provide a fantastic, one-on-one experience for dogs so they'd be still and more cooperative with me. (When there is nothing to react to, they're more likely to just chill.)
- My clients would see how happy their dog was before, during, and after their spa day and would reward me for the tender care I provided with outstanding tips.

- All the profit would go into my pocket (after deducting expenses, sales tax, and federal tax from the revenue.)
- I could further deduct expenses for the home office from our taxes (keeping more money in my pocket as opposed to being an employee.)
- I could avoid driving in traffic and spend more time with my family. (Life is short, and the independent and fit part of our life is even shorter.)
- All my tools would stay in their place, ready to use. I wouldn't break my back while packing my equipment twice per client several times a day, dragging it from and to the car.
- I could eat lunch slowly, in peace, without dog hair in it or on me while sitting on a comfy chair by the table.
- I'd have a view of my pets playing while grooming (the spa window overlooks the backyard), as opposed to looking at a gray wall. Plus, I wouldn't need to invest a lot in equipment, like cages, saving me $5–10k easily.
- I could let my pets out for pee breaks when they ring the doorbell.
- I didn't need to find groomers and bathers to hire and take on the massive responsibility of their monthly salary, training, and creating a workflow, whether the business took off or not. (I like grooming way more than coordinating people.)
- I could stay at home with my pets and Levi, making the most of life whenever there was a cancellation or break between clients.
- I could cook lunch during my lunch break (no need to prepare and bring lunch to work). I could eat healthier, and there was no need to eat out so we can save money.
- I could use my own bathroom whenever I needed to without asking for permission, and be there as long as necessary without guilt. (It sounds ridiculous to write about this in our age, but it is still a huge issue in the corporate world.)
- No need for me to buy a car to get to work. (We had only one car.)

Cons of Working from Home

- The spa room was at the end of the house, so clients would need to walk through the hallway and living room to get to the spa. I had to keep the whole house tidy. If the spa were right by the front door like it is now in the new house, I could have avoided that extra preparation daily.
- HOAs (Home Owner Associations) can make it tricky to work from home, but luckily this wasn't a real con for us, given we lived in a non-HOA neighborhood.
- I would have to have a solid rule in place to make sure I had a healthy work-life balance. (It's much easier to leave work at the salon than it is when your salon is right in your home.)

The Decision on the Final Setup

After carefully analyzing what needs of ours each option met and what they didn't, we ended up deciding that I would work from home, since that was the best fit for our case. So, we dedicated the spare room by the garage to become the doggy spa.

It was a good fit. It had a fairly large window and a door directly going to the backyard, making pee-mail breaks super easy and convenient. I could open the door or window to get fresh air anytime I wanted, weather permitting.

At this point, I had a brush, a comb, a set of nail clippers that I'd purchased, and a pair of shears that I'd won at the grooming school. I was less than ready tools-wise, but I made up for it with passion and perseverance.

Putting My Business Out There

Levi read **The Lean Startup** by Eric Ries (later I read it, too) and helped me consciously take the first steps required to start my own business from scratch. From detangling what steps to take and in what order, to understanding what was the bare minimum that I needed to start accepting clients, Levi's straightforward takes on overwhelming or tricky situations like these were truly invaluable to me.

As a minimum viable product (MVP) marketing strategy, I created a "Dog Grooming" yard sign with pink letters and paws on a white background to attract attention and put my phone number on it. I left the sign in front of the house and waited to see how it would turn out, while I was working on other to-dos of the business.

Getting My First Client

We were brand new to the state, let alone the neighborhood, so I was very nervous about how this live experiment would go with the yard sign. I had high hopes but was scared, to say the least.

Before my equipment order had arrived, I had my first client on the calendar. How?

From like ten houses down from us, a neighbor came over with her cute little mini schnauzer mix and asked about my grooming services. I was shocked and beyond happy.

I told her that I was pleased to work on her doggy, but my tools were not here yet, so we'd need a few days to make it happen. She agreed and was super happy and excited. I got her info and scheduled her on a paper calendar right there on the front lawn. How about that?!

She had a wide smile on her face as she waved goodbye and went on to continue her walk in the neighborhood with a spa day score for her cute little woofer.

I had just gotten my first client sooner than I got my business name registered or tools delivered.

I'm happy to announce I finished that initial spa day for my first client that week. It went well; I even got a nice tip! She went on to be my client for several years.

As it turns out, people enjoy the comfort of a groomer nearby, so once you show up in front of them one way or another, they'll be very appreciative of the new opportunity you provide, especially when you spice your services up with a unique philosophy they are after. Like gentle, natural, or one-on-one care.

Nowadays, social media is all about helping local businesses. You can take advantage of Yelp and NextDoor, kickstart your business, and scale it to a level that will support you financially right off the bat, whether you just got out of grooming school or want to transition from your current job to grooming solo.

Food for Thought

Getting your first client is easier than you think. Get your business out there ASAP! It doesn't matter if you don't have a website yet, it doesn't matter if you don't have business cards yet, it doesn't matter if you don't have tools yet!

Reach out, show up, and answer the questions people ask you. If you genuinely care about others and want to help them, your souls will tune in to each other, your service will likely solve a problem of theirs or many others, and they'll be grateful for you for helping them out. It may sound too touchy feely, but you can fly far and high on the wings of compassion.

Success is not about current capabilities but our mindset. Do you have a dream but feel overwhelmed and afraid of the change? Feel lost among the steps to take to get started?

Do you have people around you who don't have the capacity to support you emotionally, let alone encourage you? It's okay. You can still succeed. I am here for you.

Your dreams are precious. Share your struggles with those who can support you! If you don't have any one to talk to yet, keep it to yourself, or better yet, tell Levi and me! You can email us, and we'll give you the boost and encouragement you need to keep going. You can reach me at betty@wholesomegroomingacademy.com. We believe in you, and we will help you believe in yourself!

Chapter 3

Expanding the Client List

After I landed my first client, I took care of the legal parts of setting up my grooming business, worked on my website and logo, designed business cards, created social media pages, etc. (More about this, step by step, in part 2!)

I was hopeful and ready for new clients to start rolling in.

Social Media

Given I didn't have a lot of funds, I wanted to invest my time in generating new clients via social media and free ads. So, I tried to get out there on multiple platforms, to have a place to collect and display my reviews to build trust and generate more clients.

Unfortunately, back when I started, social media was not as booming as it is nowadays; there were much fewer options for me to choose from. Consider yourself lucky to unleash your business at this age!

If I started today, I'd go with a business account on **Yelp**, **Google**, **NextDoor**, **Facebook** (page & group), and **Instagram** to get those first clients and reviews rolling in fast.

As Levi suggested, I started doing ads on Craigslist.com three times a day. Early morning, noon, and in the afternoon or evening to catch people on their breaks at work scrolling for solutions for their dog's grooming needs. Levi told me it'd be a great way to get some traction. I wanted results but didn't have other ideas to challenge this, so I gave it a try. To my great surprise and relief, it worked. I got new clients flowing in steadily.

At this point, my grooming table looked, shall I say, "unusual." On my left side, the grooming book I used as a reference for breed hairstyles was cracked open to the chapter on the breed I was working on; my doggy client was in the middle; and my grooming tools were on the right in a pile.

I simultaneously created an account on Yelp.com and asked my clients to leave a review there. I got more and more clients, mainly from word of mouth and Yelp. They were blown away by my reviews there.

I soon realized that I had different client flow from different platforms.

Getting More of the "Easy to Work with" Clients

Yelp helped me attract not only more new clients but a different crowd than I got from Craigslist, still without investing a dollar in marketing.

Clients from Yelp were significantly more sophisticated, respectful, and didn't try to bargain all the time like my clients from Craigslist. The majority of my clients from Yelp left great tips, and their dogs were more socialized and cooperative for grooming. It made my work significantly more manageable and more fun.

After reflecting on my data and experiences with clients from different platforms, a few months in, I stopped the Craigslist ads altogether and primarily worked with the client flow from Yelp and word of mouth.

I got enough clients to fill the calendar surprisingly fast by investing a little bit of my time but still without any financially heavy marketing involved.

By about 1.5–2 months from the start, it was hard to believe, but I had proof on paper that my business was a full-time job.

So, even if you start out grooming as a part-time job or jump in as I did, you can see it is pretty simple, manageable with zero funds in marketing, and it didn't take me longer than two months to kickstart my own business.

If I started today, I am certain that with the knowledge I gained over the years, I would be able to get to my target goal within a month at most. That being said, so can you! More on this step by step in part 2.

Providing an Extraordinary Experience

Keeping Dogs Comfortable

As a grown-up, quality has always been way more important to me than quantity. I wanted to provide a spa day that was special.

I took the time to befriend the dog at the drop-off and spent more time with shy dogs until they warmed up around me and in the new environment.

No client left their dog with me at the spa without a wagging tail high above the dog's butt, standing or sitting by my side, off leash, ready for a treat to fall from the sky. Not worrying the slightest about seeing their owners leave.

I saw the instant relief in my clients' eyes when they saw my sincere efforts to help their dogs feel comfortable. Especially in those cases when I transformed a doggy's comfort level from hiding under the table in the farthest corner from me into delivering ear scratches and a resting doggy head on my lap in about 15–20 minutes.

My clients' appreciation for me comforting their dog, and the extra time I dedicated to boost canine confidence, resulted in a cooperative dog on my table without any restraint and a happy client. This made my job easier, safer, and very satisfying, reinforcing me to keep going in this direction as a solo groomer instead of giving in to the corporate setting.

Challenging Our Habits

This approach might seem too tedious and less profitable at first glance to those groomers who started in the corporate world of the industry. To some, it might even sound unimaginable to pull off.

I agree with the part that there is little to no room for handling dogs this way in a corporate setting, unless we implement radical changes to the business setup.

Most groomers learn how to groom dogs, get hired in a corporate setting, put their heads down after graduating, and work as hard as they can. They have crazy schedules, and while barely making ends meet, they forget to check in about whether this setup, pace, or place are what they enjoy or want. Sometimes they realize they don't like it, but they're worried that their investments would suffer significant losses if they threw in the towel on their dreaded business setup.

Often groomers burn out or become so exhausted that the exhaustion spills over to their quality of customer service and family life. They seem to be frustrated, impatient, and they barely have time and energy to deal with their life as is, let alone start a new one.

Meeting your needs doesn't have to be complicated, though. Bear with me because this method you're about to learn will allow you to work less and earn more simultaneously.

Making Your Dreams Come True

Imagine working in a setting where the whole spa day is designed around the dogs' and your needs and comfort! It brings on a drastic yet beneficial change that will enable dogs to relax and cooperate with you willingly. You can ditch the grooming loops altogether and even that "groomers' helper" frame above your table.

There is a work environment and business setup that will support you physically, mentally, and financially in magnitudes that you might have never imagined for yourself.

Below I will detail numbers because we groomers need to encourage each other. Understanding the possibilities of the market and sharing our prices should be standard. Employers don't encourage it because they benefit from silence about this "taboo" topic. But by talking about it, we can help each other out and set new goals based on solid examples from the industry that we are part of.

This helps for not only beginner groomers to better position themselves but also for established groomers to rethink their prices and "worth" and get those raises one way or another.

Dare to Dream Big

As for the financial part, I am the living proof that providing exclusive, one-on-one grooming, with only 5–6 hour workdays, four days a week, and having work-free weekends can yield a great work-life balance, while still supporting you well financially.

Working less and earning more allows me to spend time with my family, enjoy life, have hobbies, and rejuvenate three days a week without grooming. Yet it also enables me to make $165k a year in revenue.

After deducting a small fraction for expenses, plus sales and federal income tax, the leftover is still well above $130k per year for me to think about what to spend it on or invest it in. With cooperative dogs and respectful and compassionate clients. No back pain, no rush at work.

Daring to go with new strategies, we managed to get ourselves a serious upgrade. We purchased and moved into a house with an in-ground pool, a jacuzzi, and a spacious backyard for woofer zoomies and barefoot gardening.

The above is a radically different lifestyle that I couldn't imagine creating for myself when I graduated as a groomer. If someone had told me I could reach this far, I would have been shocked, to say the least.

Then I read a bunch of books, and I also implemented Levi's suggestions, and we got closer and closer to fulfilling the bigger and bigger dreams we came up with.

Every time I reached a new milestone, I found it a little hard to believe. But I had persevered and made my own success.

Success With or Without a College Degree

My mom could not believe the lifestyle we created for ourselves could be an option for a groomer either. She didn't think much of me after I dropped out of college two years in. She was very disappointed in me, and she kept nagging me about going back to school. But I am a stubborn one, just like she is, and I like to be the director of my own life.

I haven't graduated college, but I feel accomplished, fulfilled, and respected. We and our pets eat organic food and have a beautiful home, peace, and flexibility at work, with a trustworthy cash flow. I don't care if a college degree is not hanging on my wall. I'd much rather have a pool in the backyard for my dogs and for us.

I'm saying this to encourage my soon-to-be or already peers in the profession who might think less of themselves because they lack a college degree. Success, or fulfilling your dreams, as I like to put it, doesn't depend on whether you have one or not.

If you went to college, good for you! You can use your knowledge and complement the principles here with what you have learned to start and make your new business thrive in the new field of your choice. Having higher education like in marketing could be a huge boost for your business, and you will likely be able to perform better than I did.

When I started, no one told me I could live in a house with a pool in the backyard if I wanted to as a groomer. So, I am here to tell you that it is possible to make big dreams come true.

If traveling around the world for months is your thing, or a fancy car, or a home with a huge acreage and lots of animals, you can make it happen, even as a groomer, even if you have a chronic illness. I got where I am today while dealing with an autoimmune condition called Hashimoto's thyroiditis. In a way, it's been a blessing because it helped me put into perspective how important my quality of life is from a day-to-day view and helped me prioritize wants and needs better. It urged me to pivot my life in the direction I wanted it to go.

Of course, all this is not a competition; I'm just laying out my needs and preferences and accomplishments as an example. I encourage you to list your preferences and start your journey to make them happen!

What Does Success Mean to You?

You likely have different dreams and goals than I do. The techniques I fine-tuned throughout the years will help you make the next step after listing your dreams. Accomplishing them is right around the corner!

Starting or transitioning can seem very frightening, long-lasting, and risky. But if you have the right tools, the work you put in can be fruitful and scale way faster than you can imagine. Having a mentor as your guide to help you make decisions without learning things the hard way can be a great help to generate plenty of income for you fast.

Think about your dreams and preferences! What needs of yours do you want to meet? What would you want to accomplish that you would consider a success? Better yet, make a list and prioritize! Have a collection of needs/preferences you are unwilling to negotiate, and list some other wants that would just be nice to have.

In part 2, I will lay out a step-by-step guide to help you check off the dreams on your list faster.

Images and Videos

To take the spa experience to the next level, I took **before and after images**, along with **10–20 second videos** and **snapshots while the grooming was taking place** with my phone on a tripod. It was a "nothing fancy" setup, but it produced compelling outcomes.

I documented my furry clients watching squirrels (and later my chickens) in my backyard while getting a haircut on the grooming table. Or how they touched noses with my kitty cat, Mr. Chips, when I cleaned the table, and we took a break. These **inter-species videos and images** spiced up how unique the spa day was that I provided.

Gifting a Sweet Memory of a Fun Spa Day

While the haircut was unfolding, I shared the best of the media with the moms and dads, including the before and in-progress pictures and videos.

Sending the proof of a fun spa day to owners helped them understand the difference in their dogs' experience at my salon compared to big box salons' rushed schedules, and they saw that their investment in grooming was worth it. It was an unexpected but pleasant surprise; I even got more tips.

I saved the after images for after the checkout because I wanted the clients to see the final look of the hairstyle live at the pickup as the cherry on top.

A fine haircut looks even better when a happy dog shows it off.

Of course, later, they got the after photos to save them in their scrapbook.

The doggy clients left my salon with wagging tails and came back to me with enthusiasm to say goodbye before getting in the car. They greeted me with happy puppy jumps and even more wagging tails and kisses on their next spa day to get their fresh dose of butt and ear rubs from me while getting a haircut.

A happy dog the second time around tells a lot about the care they received the first time they got a haircut.

My efforts had come to fruition again. My clients noticed that their dogs were pulling the leash toward me the next time around and not away from the groomer and toward the car, like they did at other places. And so, they kept on coming back.

Feedback from Clients

My clients reported that their dogs loved to come to me so much; they went wild the moment they took the turn to my neighborhood. Some started calling me "Aunt Betty" and said to their dogs before getting in the car at home, "Do you want to go have a spa day at Aunt Betty's?" They saw the excitement in their dog's eyes instantly followed by jumps or zoomies. Guess what! The doggy clients knew my name.

Hearing this feedback from my clients reinforced me to stick with the low-key, one-on-one appointment business setup, no matter what.

My philosophy was challenged many times when I got flooded with new clients in springtime, and it was tempting to expand my business and hire people. I'll explain later why this setup is so powerful and why the option of growing the corporate way was not as appealing and less profitable, and seemed less fun for me.

Reflecting Back

Thinking back, I could have taken much more out of these images and videos if I shared them more frequently on social media, not with my clients only.

I was never frequent on social media in my private life, so it was hard for me to get in the habit of sharing content multiple times a day. It felt so natural to share these images and videos via text, so I kind of got stuck with it.

It worked for me. Thankfully, I still generated enough clients via word of mouth and the Yelp marketing route to overcome my lack of interest and will on this front.

Unleashing My Dog Training Skills at the Grooming Table

Expanding the wings of my training experience, I use zero grooming loops and keep dogs on the table with body language, treats, toys, and verbal requests. I subtly showed these techniques to the owners, who saw how cute and smart their doggy was for staying still. Working was fun on either end of the brush.

I'll let you in on a little secret that you may already know, but very few groomers implement it in their business. A low-distraction environment gets you halfway to a cooperative dog. Keeping a high-energy level dog still seems impossible in a busy salon, but it is not much effort in a low-distraction environment with the proper setup and mindset. If we let them sniff around to get comfy before getting them on the table, it will further improve the dogs' behavior. It is especially true when we collaborate with the owners and guide them on how to train and exercise their dogs before the spa day. Having dogs watch the "squirrel, kitty cat, or chicken TV's" live show from the grooming table keeps them entertained and cooperative while you work on them.

Need Help?

Are you having a hard time handling squirmy dogs? Check out my course "How to Keep Dogs Still for a Haircut" at: http://wholesomegroomingacademy.com

Getting New Clients Via 5-star Reviews

My furry clients got an extraordinary experience, and their owners left fantastic reviews. I was aiming for and got only 5-star reviews on Yelp, which is incredibly helpful to bring in new clients.

If someone is in the market for a new groomer, when they see only 5-star reviews, seeing others trust the business builds their trust in the business, so they're much more likely to go with the higher rated one than with the one with less impressive ratings.

If you get less than 5-star reviews, there are ways to resolve it with the client, and there are workarounds by collecting more 5-star reviews to compensate. More on this in detail in part 2!

Listening to my clients and making their experience the way they wanted it to go was a high-priority goal for me. I was combining training and grooming with natural products, which resulted in an almost instant click with clients as they were scrolling through my website. It helped me stand out from the crowd and grow my business faster. It feels incredibly good to meet other people's needs with this powerful trio, because not only do my clients like what I provide, but I offer only services that I enjoy as well.

Customer Service Skills

Furthermore, the customer service and the clients' experience make or break the deal. Even a less-than-perfect job will be much more appreciated when the care provider is compassionate and caring as opposed to when a perfect job is served with a bad attitude.

If one can run their business on the wings of empathy, they can fly far and high with this superpower.

Nowadays, people long for care and connection. If you give them the opportunity to connect with you, they will be much more likely to try out your services and they will respect you as well. Getting sued won't happen if you keep an outstanding communication flow and have the tools to discuss disputes.

In the beginning, I dedicated quite some time to the extra pampering. Then my clients seemed to love and appreciate it so much that I kept doing it and positioned the business around it.

Looking back, I didn't even know the word "positioning" in business. I went with what felt right and produced results I wanted to see more of.

New Clients Started Rolling in Without Effort

I mainly focused on getting reviews on Yelp to bring more clients to the business, since it seemed to work out well. I was tweaking the business description on my profile to capture my philosophy better, so clients could click with what kind of experience their pets would receive under my care even faster. Then they would be more likely to give my services a shot. And it worked!

Food for Thought

Regardless of the medium you are trying to get new clients from, outstanding service and customer service skills are essential to grow your business. When clients feel cared for and they find the service you provide worth their money, they will spread their experience like wildfire about your business. The conversion from word of mouth supersedes any other type of marketing strategy. The same thing applies to good and bad opinions, so put effort into making your service as fantastic as possible.

Dare to dream big! Yes, society strongly suggests you'll need to have a huge grooming salon in a mall or work for someone else to make it as an "acknowledged groomer." But there are other ways to meet your needs and stand out. A less popular one but a way more promising one. Dare to be different. One of my favorite quotes from Levi is this one:

"You might be going against the traffic, but it doesn't mean that you are going in the wrong direction."

Chapter 4

Building My Brand as a Groomer

One-on-one only, Natural, and Cage-free

As I was talking with my clients at the drop-off, they were raving about how happy they were that their pet was the only one in the spotlight and that they could come by and pick them up by the time their dog was done. This approach brought them both comfort and relief that their dog was in focus throughout the spa day, without waiting in a cage for their turn or to get picked up.

I concluded from the clients' feedback that my setup of doing one-on-one appointments only, using natural products, and not using cages attracted the most clients.

SEO – Search Engine Optimization

So, I used those phrases as the core of search engine optimization (SEO) on my website and social media sites.

- one-on-one only

- natural
- cage-free

Later, when I learned more about positioning, I realized that I naturally found a niche that enabled me to grow faster. Owners who wanted customized care for their dogs came to me in abundance.

Google Business Profile

Nowadays, many people just google their questions like "dog groomer near me," so having a Google Business account and showing up under the local radar is key. People get to see/find you faster, they can ask for directions, call/text you with a click, etc. It makes the conversation smoother from being curious to getting on the books.

People enjoy supporting local businesses, and giving them an opportunity to do so helps you and them simultaneously.

This is another marketing tip to consider when you are starting out.

Website

Generally speaking, many groomers' websites primarily function to display basic info (like contact or location) and don't share more details about services, their grooming philosophy, and images that make them stand out by providing an outstanding level of care and happy dogs.

This leaves a massive advantage for brand-new or already established, open-eyed salons to stand out with even a mediocre site, let alone a fantastic one.

Let's do a little experiment! Search for the top two dog grooming salons in your area. Then keep those tabs open and look up the fanciest websites of human spas nearby.

Most human spas have gorgeous and relaxing websites. You scroll through, and the visuals and wording take you to a place where you want to stay for a whole month even before trying out their services.

Aim to make people feel that way when they come to your website! Use those human spa designs as inspiration to capture the relaxing and rejuvenating vibe for your dog spa.

You will attract the crowd that resonates the most with the vibe you put out there. This will significantly influence your day-to-day grooming experience and profit.

Clients from Different Walks of Life

Different walks of life yield clients with different mindsets, preferences, and resources. Whether it is politically correct or not, we have a dynamic in society that we can benefit from exploring.

- People who don't have money want **quantity** (more for less).
- People who are financially established want **quality** (good product).
- Wealthy people are looking for an **experience** (quality along with tailored experience for their needs and exceptional customer care).

Most grooming salons are set up to work with loads of dogs. They are more industrialized than offering a customized experience. They choose quantity over quality, making clients pay less, and dogs, bathers, and groomers pay with comfort.

Most of the clients of those salons will come from people with less resources.

There is no such thing as cheap service. Someone always pays the difference.

I come from a relatively poor family, so I know all too well that when we got something, we didn't think about what color we wanted, or how many, but the bare minimum needed that my parents could afford. We often got clothes from relatives to avoid the need to purchase new ones. Customizing something was out of the question for us; it never even came up as an option. My parents lived and still live a "frugal" lifestyle and couldn't get out of this mindset so far. When it came to eating, for example, it was the matter of what was the cheapest that yielded the most, not about quality. It was about what filled our bellies fast with minimal prep time, not about what nourished out bodies at the same time.

Living frugally meant we always had food on the table, but the lack of quality resulted in my dad developing cancer not long after he turned fifty, my mom having thyroid issues at least since we were born, and me developing an autoimmune condition before turning thirty. So, we are paying the price now for the poor-quality food we ate decades ago.

There are things we can't afford yet, but there are also things that we cannot not afford now.

My parents had the mindset of "I can't afford it." They couldn't see far enough to understand the impact of this mindset. They were busy raising me and my sister. Weirdly enough, even after we flew out of the nest, when they had extra time and financial resources in their hands, I tried to share new avenues with them to try to improve their life, but they remained stuck in this mindset. Yes, this is a mindset issue, not a destiny. After reading **Rich Dad, Poor Dad** by Robert Kyosaki, the seed of "How can I afford it?" got planted in my head. And it was life-changing.

Let's see what different walks of life look like when we observe them from a grooming perspective! I'm speaking generally, so try not to get caught up in the nuances and instead get the essence of what I have to say!

Business Owners, CEOs, and Celebrities

In my experience, business owners, CEOs, and celebrities have a tight schedule and limited time, so they want to ensure they'll get what they want with the shortest learning curve possible. They have the funds; they desire and are willing to pay for extraordinary quality and experience. They're looking for comfort, ease, and quality for themselves and for their dogs. If something seems to be too cheap to **them**, often, they don't even give it a try because high-quality stuff most of the time comes with a higher price tag.

They have an incredibly hard time finding a customized experience for their needs in the grooming industry. The market lacks places where they feel heard and cared for the way **they want** to be cared for and the way **they want** their dogs to be cared for.

If you learn about this crowd's needs, how to attract, communicate with, and provide for this crowd, you'll be gifted with less work and significantly more money in your pocket, allowing your attention to detail to blossom year-round without burning out.

With an $8/hr price tag, financially established, let alone wealthy people didn't notice me much partially because of the price tag of my services. The quality of my work hasn't changed significantly since I raised my prices. I have more handouts to give out about coat care now that back in the day were provided as mini coat care sessions at the pickup. I upgraded the location, but the essence of my work is all the same at a $200/hr rate.

Sorting by Price from High to Low

As I became more and more financially established, I got a taste of what people were going through. I got tired of getting a cheap yet bitter experience that delayed meeting my or my pets' needs. It was especially frustrating when my pets were involved.

> # "The bitterness of poor quality remains long after the sweetness of low price is forgotten."
> ### – Benjamin Franklin

I prefer to pay more right off the bat and get what I am looking for on the first try rather than searching for a bargain, not getting the quality, doing more research, trying something else, then getting everything further delayed. Whether it was a fence project or finding a veterinarian with a quality of service that I desired, it was a massive challenge to find the right professional.

In my day-to-day life, I started sorting by price from higher to lower and by customer rating from best to worst reviews to get the quality I was looking for faster.

The loop from having a need to fulfilling it became significantly shorter with this method, and it brought relief fast and without complications most of the time.

SAHMs and People with 9–5 Jobs

Let's take a look at other segments of clients!

A stay-at-home mom of three kids might have more flexibility with the drop-off time and pickup than someone who works a 9–5 job downtown and might be more willing to work on their dog at home, yet their budget is likely more limited than a CEO's. Chances are they'll be more likely to try out lower prices first. Likely, the quality of the haircut their dog receives will make them reevaluate the quality vs. price dilemma. Seeing their dogs shiver or peeing themselves in fear at the drop-off and pulling toward the car are signs that even people possessing less empathetic skills will pick up on as crying signals for taking a closer look at the situation. A surprise short shave without a detailed explanation at the drop-off has a very similar effect even if it was inevitable due to mats or behavior.

And so on. Look at how many billions of dollars middle-class Americans spend on average on their pets annually! They invest more in their pets than they often buy for themselves. So you will see that the market is filled with opportunities. You'll just need to stop and think about which niche you prefer to go with as your primary prospect.

You can and will likely have clients from all walks of life. But it's nice to understand this dynamic and consciously choose which group of people you want as your primary prospects to get you chill workdays and financial stability. The funds you'll make will enable you to give back to your community and volunteer to help people or dogs in need if you choose to.

Build your brand as a groomer based on who your ideal client is, and you will be able to fund your life and dreams faster.

The Ongoing Grooming Industry Reform

Style and Comfort

Clients are changing the grooming industry's standards. They are no longer looking for just a haircut; they want one that keeps their dogs comfortable throughout the grooming process. Their dogs' emotional well-being is just as high of a priority (often even higher) than the importance of a gorgeous trim.

Behavior Modification

Another change is underway. A rapidly growing number of pet owners are getting way more involved in coat care at home between haircuts nowadays than ever before. They experience their dog's willingness or unwillingness to get brushed, combed, bathed, and dried between haircuts. They want prevention for undesired behavior and resolutions to transform undesired ones already showing to help their dog cooperate for grooming not only at the salon for the groomer but at home as well for them.

"Doing things to" instead of "working with" dogs, or a traumatic experience at the groomer, spills over to the grooming experience at home, whether the owners witnessed the uncomfortable or forceful grooming experience or not. They will pick up on the side effects of "factory grooming," and more and more owners are looking for a gentle and relaxing experience for their dogs.

A traumatic experience at the groomer can result in hundreds if not thousands of dollars in dog training fees that the owners will have to foot the bill for and spend their time resolving.

From this angle, it is easier to understand why owners are going the extra mile to ensure their dog gets a relaxing spa day and why it has become a higher priority for clients than solely getting a great trim. And why they are more willing to dedicate their time to put in the work and get their dogs used to grooming steps and get them exercised if they get the info in a "doable action" format of what they need to work on.

Perspective of Groomers

From the groomers' perspective, I like to emphasize to owners how important it is that they practice grooming steps and use grooming tools at home to complement and work toward an amazing grooming experience now and in the future for their dogs, themselves, and for groomers. I include notes in the "Spa Day Summary" (which I charge for) on how the doggy did at the spa day by grooming steps and include a pre-printed list of resources that the owners can practice at home between haircuts. It helps clients understand that a cooperative doggy takes more than a good groomer to create. It stands on the pillars of getting the doggy used to grooming steps at home, a good exercise before the spa day to release pent-up energy and lead to a chill day at the salon for the doggy and a great groomer.

Groomers getting a taste of the high-paced, industrialized salon vibe know all too well the tolls of working in such an environment. For example, the early starts, the long hours, the physical demands of the job, the wiggly dogs, the short or nonexistent lunch and bathroom breaks, working on weekends, the miserable or straight-up rude clients, the lack of paid sick leave, the matted dogs, being overworked and underpaid, the mean bosses or coworkers, etc. You could probably fill in many more items here that you want to change in your life sooner rather than later.

Opportunity for Groomers

Those of us groomers who see this change—the need for customized care in a low-key environment—as an opportunity can pivot their business model and can choose to ride this wave instead of ridicule it. This new approach makes a difference for dogs and owners. Groomers who dare to give it a try will thrive physically, financially, and mentally without burning out as the direct result of choosing to go with this flow.

Rapid Expansion

My business was expanding surprisingly fast, clients resonated with my vision, and I met my target goal within 1.5–2 months from the first haircut I provided. That not only kept me above the water, but also helped me pay Levi's investment back and see a potential of a higher revenue on the horizon.

Reaching my target goal was the proof I needed that I made the right choice when I put everything in the red by starting my own business.

I was finally getting comfortable with the "business owner" title at this point, enjoying the peaceful work environment at home, along with free weekends, and I had a sufficient enough cash flow to make a living with hard work, so Levi and I considered the start a success.

Little did I know that my very next challenge was dealing with so many new clients flowing in that I didn't have the capacity to work with them all.

Food for Thought

Figure out what you like to do as a groomer and position your business so it is obvious to client prospects. It's easier said than done, but there are fantastic books about it. Like **Obviously Awesome** by April Dunford and **Gap Selling** by Keenan.

Grooming books lack mentioning in detail how you can position your business. Books dedicated for businesses outside of the grooming industry are way more up to date on the strategies that are a best fit for grooming businesses in today's economy and market. Educate yourself from sources that have been recently published and use their tips to build your business.

Chapter 5

Tackling Business Challenges

Charging by the Hour

I set up my business so that I charged by the hour from the beginning. It was an essential step since I had to calculate my rates based on the time needed to work on each dog.

In the beginning, naive me just counted the net grooming time, not the extra time I discussed haircuts and behavior with owners. After I realized that I was offering a service without a price tag and that money was flowing out of my hands here, I fixed this fast.

Most grooming salons set their prices per dog. They can pull it off because if a dog needs longer drying hours, it'll be on the bather's clock, not the groomer's. A groomer's hourly rate is significantly higher than the bather's, so grooming a dog that needs a longer drying time is cheaper for the business to produce as opposed to creating a difficult haircut.

Given I, the groomer, was the only one doing every single grooming step in my business, which results in higher-quality work at the level of all grooming steps, I felt the need to charge by the hour.

Revenue Target

My goal was to match what I would have made at Wendy's per month in revenue. That goal was $800 in the first month. That was in 2013. I managed to reach $800 in revenue per month in about 1.5–2 months, which was huge. That was an immediate reinforcement for me to keep going.

Revenue vs. Profit

Levi and I didn't know how many supplies would be needed per dog, so we moderately stocked up on shampoo and conditioner, etc. and left the business to run for a month to get a feel of the costs.

$8/hr – Coupons, Supplies, Taxes

I worked at an $8/hr rate back then, using coupons. We analyzed the results after thirty days and we realized it was more like $5/hr, after deducting the coupons, sales tax, and federal income tax.

Then we realized I had expenses like shampoo and conditioner that we also needed to deduct from the hourly rate. After a hard look, I realized that less than $5/hr profit landed in my pocket. I was pretty disappointed. It didn't occur to me that I had way too low rates. I just thought that I wasn't working hard enough. We fixed this at the next redo of the business setup. (See next chapter!)

Going Back to My Old Habits

Not putting two and two together and not knowing better myself, I put my head down and worked my ass off to earn more. I kept my rates, expanded hours, along with stretching the workdays into weekends. Later I realized what a good-hearted but self-destroying move this was.

Dealing With Too Many Clients

I did 5–6 days of grooming a week, plus dealing with the scheduling daily (2–3 hours a day via email). That translated into 10-12 hours spent on grooming a day and 13–14-hour-long days, including the scheduling. I was burning out fast.

Since I had never had my own business before, I didn't know the signs to look out for that meant change was needed or could have happened. I had no idea how to know when I could raise prices or how to stick to the schedule politely with too chatty clients. How to stop clients from sitting in for the entire grooming because having the owner there was super distracting for the dog and me. Plus, it made the appointment last 2x longer than if they weren't there. Or to see it as an opportunity for offering a new service and ask them to schedule it ahead of time and pay more for the chance to be there with their dogs for the spa day to keep the appointments of the day on time.

Noticing the Signs

I learned to notice the signs the hard way. Levi was working full-time at this point for a company and navigated his startup in his spare time. He was working late, I was working late, and we missed the signs that my business could grow by only a mile, haha. I'm pretty good at hiding my exhaustion and just breaking down when I literally can't deal with the crazy high pace of work anymore. I was not helping our growth with this tragic "skill" I picked up from my parents and society.

I remember one massive breakdown of mine. It was straightforward to notice since I was silently building up to it for months. Levi offered his shoulder for me to ugly cry my soul out and talk about what was up once I calmed down enough to do so. We analyzed the situation and concluded I had tons of clients; I needed to raise prices and eliminate the coupons entirely.

Coupons and low prices helped me attract more people and get more reviews as I started, but by now they were getting in the way of my growth. I was ready for the next level.

Having enough clients is great. Having a buttload of clients and your schedule fully booked 3–4 or more weeks in advance are signs to raise your prices.

I discuss how to raise prices without worrying about losing most of your clients in detail in part two.

Building Up My Courage for a Change

I felt exhausted, overwhelmed, and frankly, I did not have the energy, creativity, and balls to raise prices, so I was fighting Levi over this. For once, in the end I was the one who had to face clients with the new price, and I didn't feel it in me to be able to stand behind a higher price mentally.

Levi had to give me a pep talk or three about it. He had multiple jobs and knew how to negotiate prices fantastically. I admired his capability to get higher and higher-paying jobs as the years went by.

I always just accepted what was offered and went on to work. I had never encountered this raising prices task until now, and it felt so new and terrifying. Instead of going for it, I entertained the thought of continuing with the current prices and suffering from the consequences a little longer just to avoid the extra challenge.

Levi helped me get over this hump and improve my mindset to gain the confidence I needed to take the next step.

Implementing Further Changes

After briefing Levi on what was up with the business, checking the data together on revenue, profit, number of new clients, and number of returning clients, we concluded that there was room to grow.

We needed to reform the business to get out of this burnout and pocket more profit. So, we made modifications on the following fronts.

Business Modifications

- Price
- Work hours

- Workdays
- Grooming tool upgrades
- Fees
- Grooming software
- Keyboard shortcuts

Prices – From $8/hr to $10/hr

We talked about taking a modest step of going from $8/hr to $10/hr. I was willing but very nervous about pulling this off. It wasn't even a 50 percent increase, but I still felt uneasy.

My mind was foggy with exhaustion and fear, and all I could think about was losing all my clients at once the moment I hit save on the new price list. It was very unlikely that I would end up with zero clients by doing this small raise, if you think it through with a clear mind. But, given my emotional state, I couldn't help but feel scared to my bones regardless.

So, I needed a mental push to make it happen, and Levi had that superpower and offered to hold my hand until I got the confidence I needed.

Ironically, when I took the step of raising my prices from $100 to $200 per hour, I was confident and excited about the change. I welcomed the outcomes, and I was no longer terrified of them. It felt like a game, not a high-stakes exam.

Work Hours

We wrote in stone that I wouldn't start sooner than 8 a.m. and would finish grooming by 5 p.m. I pledged a 1-hour lunch break from noon until 1 p.m. This new setup helped me stay on top of my meals and my thyroid health.

The workload and my "selfless" mindset up until then resulted in me skipping meals during the daytime and running on coffee and sugary yummies a lot to finish the doggies' haircuts on time and putting my health in jeopardy. Plus, we needed more time to make meals due to going gluten-free and dairy-free and other dietary restrictions per our functional medicine doctor's suggestion. Dealing with the thyroid disease diagnosis and new lifestyle hit me hard emotionally, but I kept going to make ends meet.

Workdays

We agreed that I wouldn't work over the weekends anymore to help my hands and back rest. I started to have issues with my lower back and spent a good chunk of my income on chiropractic adjustments to get me back to "normal." I couldn't enjoy even my work-free days due to the pain or just being completely exhausted.

Grooming Tools

To get back and preserve my health, I wanted a table that I could customize the height of to best fit the dog I was working on. I saw a table that I liked a lot, but it cost almost $1000. So we got a sit-stand office desk from IKEA with a grooming mat on the top as the cheapest workaround for now for around $400 instead.

Looking back, we should have made this investment right at the start to keep my back safe. It likely would have saved me the need to go to the chiropractor altogether, or at the least would have reduced the number of adjustments I needed.

New Fees

It was hard to figure out the price of shampoo and conditioner and other supplies and count the cost of the services in my head, so Levi brought up adding a new fee to the appointments. And the supply fee was born. In the beginning, there were many types of supply fees, such as for small dogs, medium dogs, large dogs, and extra-large dogs. It helped me cover my expenses for the supplies and freed me from doing too much math in my head at checkout time. It brought my clients and me clarity on labor charges and fees, but it also confused many clients, so later I switched to a flat fee for this.

At this point, my invoices included the following:

- **Labor** for the type of service provided
- **Supply fee** (for small, medium, or large dogs)
- **Sales tax**
- **Total**

Whether you are a groomer, hairdresser, makeup specialist, massage therapist, plumber, electrician, car repairman, graphic designer, etc., setting up your business by charging for labor and supplies separately one way or another is critical when it comes to knowing when and how to grow your business.

There are always supply costs involved in the service, whether it be a software subscription fee or the price of nail clippers. You will benefit from the clarity that comes with separating these expenses from labor, and you will be able to see when there is space to grow, and you can take that next step with more confidence and peace of mind.

Grooming Software

To save time on scheduling, invoicing, and at tax time, I did some research and went with 123PetSoftware to make my life easier at work. It came with reminders, easier invoicing, multiple payment methods, etc. It helped me speed up the scheduling. Before, I had been spending 2–3 hours per day on this; now, I was spending less than an hour. It was not the best solution, but it brought big relief.

Keyboard Shortcuts

I found it much easier to set up keyboard shortcuts on my phone as the skeleton of my messages than repeatedly create all texts from scratch. I customized tiny details before sending them so I wouldn't appear robotic. It helped hugely.

I had the 30-min. pickup text "pkp" set up, along with the missed call reply "mcl"—"Thank you for calling, please reach out to me via email, etc." messages (in a more extended version with links, etc.) in response to missed calls.

I added shortcuts to training videos for wiggly dogs, links for my blog posts on grooming tools, etc. and clients were blown away by the amount of info they got with a few clicks.

Conclusion

These changes helped me take a deep breath in the harboring sea of tasks and clients. They further strengthened my confidence in setting rules and boundaries, connecting with my needs, and finding ways to fulfill them.

With the extra time and energy at hand after the changes above, I had the time and energy to fine-tune the business's rules not long after this mini reform.

I learned that taking a break and rethinking where you are and where you want to go will help you get a work-life balance that fits your preferences and set you on the path to earning more while working less. Isn't that what all of us want?

Food for Thought

Remember how I worked more instead of raising prices? Learn from my mistake!

"Under pressure, you don't rise to the occasion; you sink to the level of your training."

–Anonymous Navy Seal

Train yourself to be able to figure out waves of changes before they grow too big to tackle. Read books, listen to audiobooks, attend seminars, watch tutorial videos with a critical mind. Learn from those who are making it happen, not those who are teaching it solely. Stay active on forums where they have a spirit of compassion and help.

Leave time for yourself to analyze the data from your business and come up with new plans to try to grow it. Force yourself if you "can't find time" for it.

Remember! There are things you can't afford yet, but there are also things you cannot not afford now.

You either spend time on the uncomfortable things now and resolve them, or they will come back bigger, bite you in the rear, and you will still have to resolve them but with a painfully throbbing hindquarter.

Chapter 6

Fine-tuning the Business Rules

Over time, we added even more changes to my business setup. As the months went by, we made space for frequently reflecting back on what to change and what to leave as is, and we slowly tweaked the workflow to better suit my clients' and my needs.

New Client Intake via Email Only

Given I was grooming dogs off-leash during business hours, it helped tremendously not to pick up the phone while I was grooming. It was unsafe and impractical. Lifting dogs onto the table after answering each call, even when it went down to like two feet low, was a tiring and time-consuming task and a risky business from a health perspective for me.

I decided to do all of my client scheduling via email only, and it worked out beautifully. Many people still look at me with raised eyebrows when I mention this, but it fits well in my business setup.

New Client Intake Form

I implemented new client intake forms to weed out the less passionate client prospects and understand how tricky (reactive) the dog needing a haircut was. I didn't mind working with reactive dogs at all as long as the owners were willing to train their dogs with a solid dedication to transform undesired behavior ASAP. I wanted to draw a clear line and I refused to work with clients who wanted me to solely do the behavioral transformation. It was a tough case to compartmentalize, given I love all dogs and I want to help them all, regardless of reactivity or not. However, I wanted to make a living, wanted to avoid getting seriously injured and doing rehab for weeks or months. Or getting mauled badly enough to be forced to find a new career because some owners chose not to give a hoot about their dog's level of socialization and were fine with us groomers taking on the risks and highly likely bad outcomes.

I dedicated a part for reactivity in the intake form questionnaire and got info on previous grooming behavior to get a clear understanding of the level of socialization and the client's willingness to change undesired doggy behavior. When a client had a reactive dog but was passionate about training, I was happy to help and risk my safety, given I knew it was a short-term thing and the behavior transformation was underway in a speedy manner.

Clients had to fill out a fairly long—like 4ish letter-sized pages—form online and send it back to me before scheduling an appointment.

The less passionate ones didn't fill it out at all, so I further filtered the highest and most dedicated clients without much extra effort on my end.

Agreement Form

It is essential to have a well-constructed pet release form from the business's perspective. I implemented an agreement that every new client and I signed on paper.

It is an agreement between the client and the business owner about the rules of the business and ways to resolve disputes, how to deal with injuries, etc. It includes resolutions to situations like when the dog gets dropped off late or when a dog gets injured at a place. Both parties sign the agreement before any grooming takes place to ensure clarity and accountability.

Initially, this agreement form was on paper; then, I migrated the form online to be signed and stored in the scheduling system, after I upgraded to a software that supported it.

And today it is implemented in our CRM system, Pet Groomer App.

30-min. Pickup Notice

I implemented a 30-min. text message notification to inform my clients when I expected them to come back, and it worked wonders to keep my schedule smooth. Most of them were very respectful, keeping in mind the pickup time perfectly.

This "pkp" notice sounds like this: "Hi Cassie. :) Roger is doing amazing. :) He's such a cute and cooperative guy! I could not challenge him today. He did great even for the pawdicure part. He met with Mr. Chips and both were very polite when sharing kisses. (image included) Roger is going to be done by 2:15 pm. The total is going to be $120 for today's spa day. I can take cash, check, cards, ApplePay, Venmo (link). See you when you get here! :) "

Payment Methods

- Cash
- Check
- PayPal (new)
- Google Pay (new)
- Venmo (later)
- Apple Pay (later)

At the beginning I accepted cash and checks only, no cards. Then as my client base grew, there was a bigger and bigger need for the comfort of card payments, so I obliged. PayPal and Google Pay were my initial go-tos.

Then one of my clients introduced me to Venmo and I liked it a lot. And when I switched from Android to iPhone, I started taking ApplePay as well.

Most of my clients pay either before or after the pickup via an app, or via cash or check, making the pickup super fast and easy. I like checks, Apple Pay, and Venmo best due to no fees.

It's incredibly easy to set up the digital payment methods. And it's especially convenient if you have a CRM software (customer relations management) to keep track of who paid with what payment method and how much.

A good software makes tax time a breeze, especially when you have an accountant to go over your data.

Late Pick-up/Drop-off Fee

I remember being a rookie of the team at the beginning of my career at salons and when a client didn't show up on time, I was the "dedicated candidate" by older staff members to stay late and I hated it. One time I was supposed to get off at 5 p.m. and the client didn't show up until 8 p.m. They got no repercussions from the business owner, I was in no position to have a say (at least I thought so), I didn't get extra payment for the longer workday to compensate the discomfort of the evening, and the clients kept coming late. That was not a business setup I wanted for myself at all. I wanted clarity, accountability, and respect for all parties.

A few clients couldn't care less about being there on time for their appointment regardless of the reminders and notices I sent them. Given how hard it was for me to deal with dogs from different households if there was overlap and the discomfort that came over me that they seemed to not respect my time and me, I added a new fee per Levi's suggestion.

I started charging late pickup/drop-off fees by the minute, with the same rate as if I were grooming. I added it to the agreement form that they signed, so it wasn't a secret.

It soon cleared up the owners' errors and compensated me for their learning curve of respect. I even lost a few clients to this. I felt sad for losing the doggy client but got the relief of a smoothly running business.

Last-minute Cancellation Fee

I also added a fee for last-minute cancellations. This was another way to help clients prioritize my time, letting me know of any foreseeable change or taking responsibility for an unforeseen event.

For example, if they let me know 48 business hours in advance of a change, no fees were added. If they canceled in less than 48 business hours, the fee was applied. I set it to be 50 percent of the canceled appointment's total. It worked. Given most human hair salons charge you the whole thing if you don't show up, I felt 50 percent was still very generous.

Plus the scheduling software sent out a reminder three days in advance, so my clients had everything at hand to comfortably change the date or time of their appointment without the fee.

I waived the fee for those very few clients who wished not to pay it and banned them from the establishment. I labeled the expense in my head as a donation for peace of mind. It brought me relief and clarity that it would not happen again.

Conclusion

The day-to-day work was effortless at this point. I was getting more experience in grooming and customer care; the client flow was steady and comfortable; the rules were designed to aid relaxed and cooperative dogs yet kept in mind my needs as well. I was a happy camper, and so were my furry clients and their owners.

Food for Thought

Your grooming business is a huge negotiation game. If you get the hang of it, it'll serve you well. You offer services and prices that your clients will consider. You offer rules that your clients consider. They might ask for new services that are not on your list, but you can put it there if you listen carefully enough with the right price tag instead of calling them crazy.

You can sabotage your life by not holding on to the bridle and giving up on your comfort and safety. Your mental or physical health will give you a red flag or you will realize it at some point by going broke or not growing financially enough to your standards out of kindness toward the world without considering your own needs on the same level as others'. It can be as serious as a medical issue that you'll need to foot the bill for or a vacation you choose to pass on.

I've been to all of these stops in life and the ride helped me realize where I'd like to be and take steps toward a more desirable future with urgency.

The choice is yours to make your life go in the direction you want it to go.

The next chapter is filled with super important info, so please, regardless of the emotions the title might bring up in you, give it a chance to learn from my experience.

Chapter 7

Specializing in Doodles

Getting Better at Positioning My Business

I read a lot about marketing, but the book that brought the most significant impact on my business's growth was the one titled **Obviously Awesome** by April Dunford. I was carefully reading the printed version to soak it in as much as possible, highlighting it and taking notes, given that the audiobook was not available yet to put it on loop like I usually do nowadays. I realized I needed to help my client prospects better understand why my services were extraordinary. I realized I was offering Hilton™ quality for the Motel 6™ price range. So, I concluded I had to phrase my services differently on my website.

Keeping Space for Autonomy

To this I added my own kind of spice. I hated when someone was pushing stuff on me in my personal life like at a store or at the market, so I presented my suggestions as suggestions, not upselling. I explained why I suggested what I suggested, like if the client wanted a 2-inch long coat left on the dog but the dog was matted to the skin all over, I showed them the mats. I asked them to feel it, to try to find the skin in the sea of thick mats, to try pulling the thick mats apart, and I made them realize and experience how bad the coat quality was and that there was no other humane option but a short shave.

I offered them to get a second opinion and gave them space to decide for themselves. I told them what I could do on their dog and why I won't torture a dog with impossible dematting, and I offered them the relief to never get there by following my guidance in the handouts.

They much appreciated the insight and the space I kept for their autonomy to do its thing. Clients understood when a short shave was necessary and were happy with even the short buzz cut for this time. They were hopeful and dedicated that it would never happen again because they got a folder from me with handouts on coat care and could learn how to avoid it from now on.

Setting expectations instead of a surprise short shave was appreciated and kept my business's 5-star rating.

Exploring Niches by Breed

I had only one dog, a Malinois, at this point. Not the most popular breed for groomers. Haha. They are famous for their short hair and crazy energy, so it is a popular police and military breed.

Back in Europe I used to help train police and military dogs for bitework. And I fell in love with the short-haired version of the Belgian shepherd. I enjoyed the dogs' desire to work with me, their fast response, and raising a "Maligator" helped me build up some tricks on how to level with their speed and keep high-energy dogs engaged, cooperative, and still for a spa day.

I enjoy grooming my fur missile and other high-energy dogs, and helping them cooperate with me for grooming was pretty much effortless. In my low-key environment, combined with my tricks in training, treats, toys, and requested exercise at home before the spa days, I managed to groom them with ease while having fun with them.

Dogs who didn't do well at other spas got close to or simply perfect report cards at "Aunt Betty's Spa."

Many groomers get overwhelmed by the energy doodles have and how dangerous and uncomfortable it is for people to work with wiggly dogs in a high-paced salon environment. Many doodles get a short shave to "get the spa day over with fast" or because of deep mats present due to uneducated owners, sadly without a detailed explanation or any coat care suggestions at salons. The poor fellas get a "recurring" shave. Saying "Brush your dog more!" ain't gonna cut it. Clients (not just doodle clients but especially them) need to know how to exercise and handle their dogs, what tools to use and how, learn to differentiate between brushable and not brushable mats, know the grooming work-flow "brush before the wash," etc. As a result, more and more doodle owners found me and ended up at my salon to get a pretty trim and info on coat care.

Most groomers don't have a coat care training implemented in their services, though it would be very helpful. It's a win-win if you charge for it. Most likely a double win for you, because the client will pay for the training service and you'll get to work on a cooperative and mat-free dog later. Now this can be a handout, a blog post, a video, or an in-person mini-lesson.

Breeders have limited knowledge on coat care and sometimes, let's face it, they spread ideas that makes every groomer's skin crawl. Like "Don't get your doodle groomed before one year of age!" etc. Vets and vet techs understandably have no idea about breed-specific coat care; they are specialists of another profession.

But we groomers do know the details, and we need to help owners do better by sharing our knowledge with them. Given how busy we are, it has to come with a price tag. The owners will be happy to pay for this service, just have it as an option to offer. It's fun to take a break from grooming and enjoy a talk with clients rather than stressing our backs at the table or by the tub all the time. And it's a paid "vacation" if you play it right.

In my practice, the vast majority of doodle owners were super kind and caring and had tons of questions about coat care between haircuts. I was happy to help them with that before or after the spa day, as my schedule allowed. I got more and more doodles as clients by word of mouth, as they shared with other doodle pawrents at the park how their spa day was with me. Showing off the styles sealed the deal.

I enjoyed working with doodles, loved their hairstyle and personality, their owners were kind and curious, I was having fun explaining coat care suggestions, and they left great tips; something wonderful was in the cooking.

Doodle Day

One day I had only doodles on the calendar for the day, and I told Levi how cool it was and that I wished it was like this every workday. As always, his response hit me right in the feels. He asked, "What if you specialized and groomed doodles only?" I could not believe my ears, and since I'd never heard a groomer specialize in a breed to that extent, I responded with a long and loud laugh. His serious face made me stop after a while, and when I finally shut up, he told me, "I'm serious."

It was at this point that I considered it an option. But, just as with any new direction in the first few years of my career, I needed time to befriend this opportunity. But soon enough, I made the decision, and I was taking only doodles as new clients to give the theory a safe test run.

With this change, I not only worked actively toward grooming only my favorite breed, but also found a new niche with outstanding resources.

Many groomers dread working on doodles because of "energy and mats." But they are really not that difficult to work with in a low-key environment and with the right setup to train the owners on coat care.

Embracing the Doodles

A few months after taking on only doodles as new clients, I noticed something exciting about the percentage of tips I was receiving. Doodle people were leaving $20–30–40 tips regularly. Once I showed my data to Levi, we knew we were going in the right direction, and tremendous opportunities were right around the corner for my business.

We realized that we'd found a group of people that I could easily connect with and who had better resources than the owners of any other breeds I'd encountered. I got a few great tips from owners of other breeds, but never had I seen a more generous group of owners than doodle owners. Let alone a large enough group that I could specialize in them solely.

I always admired people who had the funds to keep horses, and it felt like I connected with a similar crowd who owned dogs instead. They got a large breed; they managed to foot the bill for a $2000–$5000 puppy, feed them high-quality food, and cover vet and frequent grooming bills for a lifetime.

When I was a kid, we got a dog for free from a friend's backyard because they had puppies. And the dynamic hit me again.

When financially established or wealthy people want a dog, they'll go on an adventure and exploration, compare breeds, looks, and behavior, get a better understanding of breeders' work, genetics, and check the price tag. For them getting a free puppy is likely not appealing as much as getting one that fits right into their lifestyle and family without loads of desensitization due to improper upbringing or unfortunate trauma of the dog.

Don't get me wrong, rescuing pets is very altruistic. But we need to face the fact that adoption can often result in getting a dog with loads of undiagnosed medical or unnoticed behavioral issues that take a long time to correct—if they can be corrected at all—and loads of money to sponsor and time to resolve. A reputable breeder of any breed does detailed genetic testing and uses the dogs with the best genes only and socializes the puppies so they'll take on life's challenges in a balanced and confident way.

Most doodle owners in my location have white-collar jobs and thrive in the corporate world, being rocks of the society and their community. They have lots of friends; they arrange doggy play dates, birthday parties for their doodles, etc. And guess what breed of dogs their friends have? Doodles. I got into a crowd where they shared my philosophy about canine care, and my work's quality spread like wildfire via word of mouth.

To catch up with the demand, I soon had to raise my prices by 50 percent and then 100 percent to make the most of the service-demand ratio.

Food for Thought

When clients present something to you, regardless of the way they do it, if you listen carefully enough, you'll find a need behind it for them, and for you. And can embrace this need and make the most of it with a win-win solution. Like I did with the Skip the line! fee or with the Late drop-off/pickup fee, as I'll discuss in the next chapter.

I'm not saying you have to become a doodle specialist like I did, though that'd be awesome since there is a need and plenty of room for you to become one. You can find clients with an abundance of resources through other methods besides specializing in one breed. I love doodles with all their fur and energy and it was an unplanned surprise to end up going this route, but it worked out well for me.

The essence of what I'm saying is you can turn even seemingly unpleasant situations around and grow your business and earn respect along the way.

Solo groomers with a low-key environment and customized services are much needed in the industry for any and all breeds.

I sincerely hope you consider the opportunity to become one.

Chapter 8

From Double to Triple Figures

After my Hashimoto's diagnosis, my need for health, peace, and a smaller workload skyrocketed, and along with Levi's guidance, I worked up the courage to work even less and ask more for my services.

Levi's suggestions were always my main influence. But there were other people in my life who, though they didn't have any direct insight into my business, inspired me to change my mindset and positioning of it.

Influencers

Dr. Aviva Romm

One of them was my doctor. It took me five doctors until I got a proper diagnosis for my symptoms, and it was tiring to find a skilled doctor who listened. After many years and lots of disappointment and research, I found Dr. Aviva Romm, MD and her functional medicine practice[1] specializing in women and children's health. I read her blog posts, ordered her books, bought her course, and made an appointment.

----

1   http://www.avivaromm.com

I had to fly from Austin, TX, to Manhattan, NY, to meet her. I put all my coins from the piggy bank into this trip and it was SO worth it. She listened to my symptoms, didn't brush off any of them like the previous MDs did. She wanted to know about the full picture, including my upbringing and lifestyle, to know what to test for and how to get me better with the least amount of medications possible, as fast as possible.

I remember the initial appointment was scheduled to last 1.5 hours, and I started crying after a few questions about my childhood. I was crying throughout almost the whole session; I was a hot mess. Dr. Romm gave me the warmest hug and a box of tissues to get me through the appointment so she could help me. She listened and asked and listened and asked. I've never had doctors take this much of time with me and show true curiosity and the deepest intention to help me get better. She got the info that she needed, she checked my vitals, and suggested a load of tests based on my history and current health complaints. We had a follow-up after receiving the lab results and she helped me get my life back.

I liked it a lot that she is an MD, herbalist, and a midwife. Taking advantage of both natural and western medicine, she customized my care, and got my life back to the energetic and creative level I had hoped for.

Her philosophy inspired me to provide the same detailed care to my clients in my doggy spa and bring out the best in their dogs, naturally. To tailor the services to their needs and find resolutions that fit the whole family's lifestyle. By joining training, grooming, and the heart of a dog mom, I found I could provide for my clients a detailed level of care in multiple aspects of their needs.

I've been to so many other doctor's offices that I had to realize there are huge differences in services from GPs, specialists, and functional medicine. No doubt, functional medicine doctors charge a higher price, but they will help you heal fast, resulting in a more enjoyable life and fewer doctor's visits. They don't let insurance companies bind their hands by allowing some and not allowing many needed tests and preferred supplements or medications.

Functional medicine doctors don't take insurance at all, but they order the tests that you need and what you want. I felt I would much rather pay a higher price for a doctor's visit and get well sooner, than go from one doctor to another and not get the results I was looking for and continue feeling miserable for a bargain. It was so worth the price! The value I got for the money I invested highly superseded the expenses I footed the bill for.

"Functional Dog Grooming"

It is a very similar case in grooming. Just because someone owns a "groomer" title, it doesn't necessarily mean dogs feel comfortable or are safe in their care. We've all heard crazy stories where dogs got bitten or horribly injured or even died under a groomer's "care."

This deeply caring experience is the one I wanted my clients at the spa to have. A "functional grooming experience" where the dogs are free of cages and the groomer's hands are not bound by corporate rules but are free to provide customized care to their clients. A practice that not only provides beautiful trims, but one that meets the dog's needs and fits their lifestyle, yet also includes the dog's comfort as the highest priority while getting a trim or a soak. An approach that also keeps in mind the dog's behavior, and helps the dog feel cared for and stay calm, while getting a haircut.

Marshall B. Rosenberg

I had a fairly rough upbringing, and Marshall's work introduced me to a formula for peace. I read his book titled **Words are Windows, or They're Walls** in Hungarian in high school. It has been the biggest pillar and most useful tool to bring peace to my soul. His work helped me understand what compassion is and gave me a recipe for how to generate it in my life, toward myself, to have enough for others as well. His method is the most precious method I've learned in my entire life.

You can read about his work and dozens of books on "Giraffe language" on his publisher's website puddledancerpress.com.

The Flow of Raising Prices

It took a while for me to stand behind the growth mentally and have the confidence to charge more and more for my services, but I got better and better at tackling this challenge. I think the biggest help was understanding how deeply customized my services were and how it makes me stand out from the crowd.

There were multiple ways I chose to raise prices. Here is the backbone of how I raised my prices rapidly.

1. **Getting better at positioning my business** (helping people see the value)
2. **Exploring niches by breed** (specializing)
3. **Exploring niches by resources** (specializing)
4. **Adding more services and applying more fees** (honoring the market's need)

I had to work a lot on my mindset to deal with this topic of raising prices. I knew that I did an impeccable job with all my heart and that the dogs were super happy while getting groomed, but I just could not stand behind the idea of new prices for a while mentally.

Now that you know the backbone of how I did it, let's take a closer look at the actual steps of getting from $8/hr to $200/hr. You read the $8/hr to $10/hr already, so we'll pick it up from there.

From $10 to $15/hr

Periodically, Levi and I took a look at the data, and we compared and analyzed the following reports:

- Number of all clients

- Number of returning clients
- Number of new clients
- Number of inactive clients
- % of tips per clients
- Revenue vs. profit

When about 75 percent of clients left at least a $10–$20 tip, we felt comfortable that there was room to grow. Given how scaredy-cat I was, we went from $10/hr to $15/hr next. Clients took it without any issue. A small percentage of clients (less than 5 percent) tipped less than usual or didn't tip at all after the price increase.

The new doodle clients rolled in steadily, so I was way better off with the raise even though I lost a few tips compared to before. This was around springtime, so I was a busy groomer but still comfortable with the workload.

From $15 to $20/hr

During summertime, I got off track and the workload reached an unbearable volume, and I was back to 12–14 hour workdays. I was getting exhausted again, fast. We got another can't miss "meltdown reminder," and Levi pushed me to raise my prices again.

I was worried because I'd raised prices this year already, and I was terrified again that I'd piss off my clients and all of them would leave the moment I changed the price list.

Levi asked another eye-opening question that hit me hard: "Where is it written down in stone that you can change your prices only once a year?"

I was like, "You got me." Then I proceeded to tell him the same worry that I had before, about clients leaving in masses. Plus, I had to be the one who'd go in front of the clients with the new price tag on my services.

He sat me down, showed me the data, and reassured me that even if a quarter of my clients left, which was very unlikely, I still would be totally fine without losing money, given the number of new clients rolling in.

He pointed out that I got amazing tips as proof that clients love my work, and the majority of them were not going anywhere due to a $5/hr (~$10 per grooming bill) raise in prices because I was worth way more than that to them. The worst would likely be only getting a few less tips. I saw the compelling data, but I was still afraid.

It was around this time when I saw the TED talk **Fake It Till You Become It**[2] by Amy Cuddy.

After watching it, I took a deep breath and agreed with Levi's plan. I redid the prices page on my website that day, and faked it until I became it. The following day, I started my day watching that video like three times to make it stick. I started charging the new price the next month, so I had some time to build up my confidence before I had to go in front of my clients face to face with that price tag on my services. It gave me time to watch that TED Talk a few more times, and I even did the power poses suggested by Amy to work up my courage for the first few days of the next month.

The change went well. Just like before, I came out of it way better off financially, and I worked and lived a comfortable life again.

From $20 to $30–40/hr

Next spring came, and after this comfortable phase of grooming for $20/hr, I found myself underwater again. I was working 12–14 hours again, and I didn't even notice. A meltdown let me know how overworked I had become. Again. It was ridiculous at this point, since I'd already done this three times and still couldn't pick up on the signs soon enough to catch the load of work before it reached an insane level and it broke me down.

I sat down with Levi, and after crying my soul out again, we went through the most immense hardships I was facing. We figured the two major issues were the number of clients I was taking on and the scheduling duties.

---

2   https://www.youtube.com/watch?v=RVmMeMcGc0Y

We read **Rich Dad Poor Dad** by Robert Kiyosaki around this time, and we realized a few major perspectives that helped us come up with a solution.

I needed help, and I was providing a service that attracted clients in such a magnitude that I had to raise prices again. So, we made a more complicated move than before.

Three-fold Change

1. **Hired help** for doing the schedule – 1–2 hr/day (so I could rest right after work)
2. **Added a new fee** to cover the costs of the help (admin fee)
3. **Raised my prices in tiers**
   1. $30/hr for **existing clients** (from $20)
   2. $40/hr for **new clients** (from $20)

This tier system helped us understand the market better and avoid a setback if we went too high with the guessing of the price. I felt safer with this method and thought we had a well-thought-out plan. I almost felt comfortable with this.

Saying Goodbye

Raising the price went very well, with no significant setback. A few unicorns (super kind clients from the "Craigslist ads era") couldn't keep up with this price, so we had to say goodbye to each other. It was hard on them and me emotionally. I really wanted to help them, but I had to realize with the lower price range, I wasn't going to meet my need for buying a better house in the near future and improving my life.

I encountered this situation later several more times, and the compassion and care for those beloved clients inspired me to create the **Coat Care for Pawrents** course and series.

This enabled me to help those with less funds get their dogs groomed "Aunt Betty's way" and helped me earn a high enough income to fund my desired future through grooming.

Hard-to-Swallow Pill

I realized that if my goal was to buy my dream house sooner rather than later, I had to come up with the price for it. Along with that, I had to face the fact that I was responsible for providing extraordinary service, and my clients could choose to go with my services and prices and come up with the money for it, or do it themselves via my courses, or go somewhere else for a haircut. I did my best to help them with their grooming needs, but I could not offer more than my new prices or an alternative DIY grooming course by myself without compromising my own needs.

Selfish, Selfless, Self-full

Marshall Rosenberg's work helped me understand and fire up feelings of compassion toward others and find solutions that would meet others' and my needs as well. I didn't want to be selfish, but I was literally and figuratively sick of being selfless and suppressing my own needs. I wanted to meet everyone's needs and be "self-full," how Marshall Rosenberg puts it. To have enough compassion within me for others and myself at the same time.

Compassionate communication showed me that I am responsible for my future and that others are responsible for theirs, and we can help each other along the way up to a comfortable extent.

Strategy to Meet Needs

The **Rich Dad Poor Dad** book helped me find financially beneficial strategies that helped my business grow faster. I had to face the fact that

I could choose to charge less and delay establishing myself financially and buying a house. Or I could choose to charge more and contribute to buying a home for us. I wanted to have a house of my own, so I buckled down.

From $30–40/hr to $40–60/hr

From then on, when clients started flowing in and my schedule started filling up fast, my assistant kept an eye out and let me know that the schedule was getting crazy. So, I had the reminder on time, avoided the meltdown, and pivoted the business more smoothly and effectively.

The time soon came again when clients were flowing in massively. And I had to think about raising the price again.

We raised the prices in tiers from now on, so I came up with the $40–60/hr price per Levi's push. I started calling him my financial advisor at this point. Haha.

Old clients went up from $30/hr to $40/hr, and the new clients went up from $40/hr to $60/hr.

It went smoothly. I was growing steadily. A few clients dropped out again, but nothing close to shaking the business in the slightest.

I gave a couple of months for this price to settle in before I was confident enough to take a unique step in the grooming industry. I don't know any other groomer or facility that has pulled this off to date.

Specializing in the "Doodle Breed"

At this point, about 75 percent of my clients were doodles. Levi pushed me to go doodles only. I knew he was right; I bit my tongue and asked my assistant to send out a newsletter to non-doodle owner clients informing them that I was specializing in doodles going forward, and we needed to say goodbye. It was a bit easier this time since my assistant dealt with any disagreement from clients.

It was an emotional move. I kept a few of my favorite non-doodle breed clients in secret, but 99.9 percent of my clients were doodles after this move.

This step helped me free up some space, so the holiday rush was at a comfortable pace. My schedule for the least three months of the year was booked about 2–3 weeks ahead. That enabled us to find a spot at a reasonably soon enough time for new clients, and I got to work with my favorite breed every single day.

From $40–60/hr to $60–80/hr

I was living the dream. My work-life balance was fantastic; I thrived physically, felt comfortable mentally, and made enough money to put in the piggy bank that made a difference.

I had free time, so I was more active on forums, read/listened to more books, and watched videos about various business topics. Two books inspired me tremendously.

One was **Your Second Life Begins When You Realize You Only Have One** by Raphaelle Giordano. My assistant suggested the book to me. It resonated with me because the more relatives passed away in my family, the more I felt the need to make the most out of my life and do it consciously.

Then I read the book **Get Rich, Lucky Bitch: Release Your Money Blocks and Live a First-Class Life** by Denise Duffield-Thomas. The subtitle of this book clicked with me better than the title itself. I never longed for golden sofas, $100k+ cars, or to live in a mansion, but after reading this book back to back, I entertained the thought of having a pool in the backyard.

One fascinating technique Denise shared is that you are not asking a high enough price if you don't blush when saying it out loud.

At first, I laughed it off, and then I said my current hourly rate out loud, and I didn't blush at all. Then doing the exercise in the book, I went higher and higher until I did. This became my go-to method as the primary gauge of the right price. Then, of course, I carefully analyzed the business data and timed it mindfully to play it safe.

At this point, I further tweaked my website to "justify" the raise in my mind and to fine-tune the content a bit, update the images, etc.

It was at this point that I realized when I heard about people making more than me, I didn't get all grumpy or jealous like I did as a kid about grades or sports achievements. I felt the juice and dedication spread in my body, the freedom to pivot my life in my own pace in the direction I wanted it to go. Other people's experiences were purely inspirations, without any hint of disappointment in myself as opposed to when I was a kid.

Reddit Forum

I found a thread on r/doggroomer where a freshly graduated groomer student was asking about the prices groomers charged/worked for to get a better understanding of their "market value."

I was grooming $40–60/hr at this time and as I was scrolling through the replies, I saw someone who provided a one-on-one grooming service in San Francisco, CA, and charged $80/hr. It was inspiring. I decided to change the price to get in the game again.

I comfortably set the price to $60–80/hr for old/new clients. Everyone took it without any issues. I was expecting some resistance, but ended up almost disappointed within a few weeks because even though I blushed about the price, it seemed I'd targeted a too-low price range and I could earn more.

From $60–80/hr to $80–100/hr

The day came when my calendar was filled up again, so it was time to work up a new price. So, I did the blush test and came up with an $80-100/hr rate. I WAS BLUSHING. Holy crap. I felt excited and energized, but oh boy, was I worried. Triple figures for a groomer! Mamma Mia!

Funny enough, clients took it the exact same way. A few left, many more new ones came, and there was a significant change in revenue and profit. I started earning considerably more because the $100/hr clients were rapidly getting closer to outnumbering the old clients.

I was very worried about the next raise. The three-figure hourly rate made me super happy, but I could not think about the next raise without blushing—not even thinking about a number.

Levi kept bugging me about it. He randomly asked when I would raise prices again. I told him I was still blushing, so don't ask me for another two months.

Several months went by, and the number of new clients started rolling in again in masses. My calendar was getting more and more full, and I had to get to it again and do something.

I made $85k with this price tag that year and it satisfied my need for now. This was the most I had made so far to that date. I really did not feel comfortable even thinking about raising prices from here, let alone thinking about a specific number. I found another money block to work on. I told Levi all my excuses, like I was already at $100/hr, so it was okay to not raise the price any more. I don't have a college degree; how could I ask for prices even higher than this?

He asked me, "Where is it written in stone that professionals without a college degree can't ask for more than $100/hr? Even if it was written in stone, aren't you someone who challenges these "traditions"? You came to America alone when you were twenty-two years old and didn't listen to anyone who didn't believe what you believed in. Where is that Betty now? Don't get stuck at your money blocks just because people around you are not asking for more in your profession. Dare to lead the way!"

That question about "the Betty with balls" hit me right in the feels. I started wondering about that myself. I found myself playing it safe. Growth, as we know, won't happen in our comfort zone. I was going back and forth about it for a while. Comfort and financial stability vs. taking up a challenge and finding even more stability. I wanted to feel challenged and accomplished again and grow.

$100/hr for New and Old Clients

I finally gave in and said to him that I was willing to do $100/hr for all my clients but nothing else. I felt I had to rest at this milestone a bit more mentally, so I told him to leave me alone again for a while about this.

Skip the Line! Fees

When the COVID puppies started emerging to an extent that we got an insane rush of new clients, my assistant knew we were saving money like mad for a new house, so she booked the calendar full in my business hours and didn't let me know when we were booking out further than 3–4 weeks—a bit of a communication oopsie on my part.

I was so busy working I didn't do the general checkups of the next month's schedule ahead of time, and we realized too late that we were almost fully booked out 2-ish months in advance, and we barely were able to find a spot for our recurring clients within 4–6 weeks for a 30-minute Face, Feet, Fanny trim during regular business hours, let alone for a two-hour long "The Works" appointment.

I was very worried about how I would be able to get out of this hot mess with my prestige left intact.

Levi chimed in, and we came up with the following action plan.

Saving the Schedule Plan

- For about two months, for old clients, I would do before/after business hours appointments, and I'd suck it up to avoid returning clients leaving.
- We'd implement Skip the line! fees (on top of the grooming bill) for those new clients who wanted to come earlier than we had a spot in regular business hours (2-ish months out). This way we didn't have to say no to them and they had the option to come earlier. We wanted to test out this theory.

- Skip the line! fee for 60-min. appointments – $100 flat fee
- Skip the line! fee for 120-min. appointments – $200 flat fee

I had a very profitable few months with a crazy workload, making over $16k per month. I was thrilled with my bank account but was tired enough to think about the next price move.

The number of people who paid the Skip the line! fee and ended up with a $450–$550 grooming bill for a single dog for a single spa day was confirming our theory: there was room to grow even from here.

From $100/hr to $100–200/hr

Levi noticed he got better results and faster responses from me after a long, profitable day when I was super tired. So, on one night like this, he approached me again with the question, "When will you raise your prices?"

Given that I was ready to get the physical relief and financial boost of a new and doable workload that followed each raise, I said, "Okay, let's talk about it!" This is how the conversation went:

Levi: How much will you ask for per hour?
Betty: I don't know.
Levi: How about $120/hr?
Betty: I'm not going to rewrite the pricing page for a $120/hr raise. (In my defense, I was super tired and cranky. I tend to express myself more "raw" than compassionate when I am exhausted.)
Levi: Okay. I like it! How about $150/hr then?
Betty: Hm. $150. I like it, but I'm not blushing saying that out loud.
Levi: How much then?!?!
Betty: Well, $200. I'm blushing for sure. $200/hr for the new clients it is!

My confidence didn't last too long. By the time I went to edit the pricing page, I did the update with shaking hands and an awkward laugh out of disbelief over what I was about to pull off. I was doubling my hourly rate from $100 to $200. I finished the pricing page, hit save, and closed the tab as fast as I could. It was hard to face this new money block. Sometimes, not only dogs but us humans need some desensitization as well. So, I got to it and worked on my mind.

Clients started rolling in at a manageable pace with the new rate, and I had the conversions I needed to enjoy a significant and ongoing bonus. I felt accomplished, acknowledged, and respected. People recognized me and valued my work enough to be willing to pay crazy high prices (to my "old" wallet and way of thinking) for my services.

As you can see, setting your own prices as a solo groomer has a totally different scale than asking for a raise in the corporate world. I hear from so many groomers who work their butt off in long shifts and a crazy work environment, who have to ask for permission to go on a pee break, that they are terrified of asking for a $3–5 raise out of fear they'll be fired or at best denied.

Illusion of Safety

So many people are trusting a company to take care of them, no matter what. Let me tell you a hard thing to swallow. The moment the company has plans and you're not a part of them, they'll fire you without a blink. Working for someone is an illusion of "job safety." I trust myself to get my own clients way more than I'd trust a company to keep my job and give me a raise at a scale that I'd like my salary to move up.

Being your own boss and setting your own rules enables you to get where you want to be WAY faster than in the corporate world, while having fun.

I always joke when I take a break when "I'm not supposed to" that, "Well, I can take a break, I have a very kind and understanding boss." It cracks up Levi all the time.

4-Day Work Week

I needed more time to focus on my courses and books, so given the bonus I got with the new raise, I wanted to groom less. I dedicated Mondays to be "digital days" so I would have time to finish my projects and have another stream of revenue. It worked wonders for my mental health and creativity. I feel like it is a 3-day weekend, yet I still get the progress I desire for my "side projects" like this book.

Or, if I am very tired, I take all three days off and get undisturbed rest. It's like a mini vacation.

New Service – Dry Cut Only

After the initial springtime client flow, enough of the new clients showed signs that the $200/hr price range was a bit pricey that it made me think. The urgent need for them to get a haircut by me justified the Skip the line! fee, but once they were on the schedule, quite a few asked about how they could lower the grooming bill.

The conversion of new clients slowed down to a comfortable level, so it was a relief with two sweet layers. It was nice since the hours of scheduling doubled before the raise, and I had to pay overtime for my help to go through emails, and the number of scheduled appointments was lower. The new price helped people decide whether it was to their liking or not before reaching out.

We still were able to fill the calendar without any issue for 1–2 weeks in advance, but I felt the need to figure out something that would bring me some ease and help more new clients get on the books to improve the ratio between the $100–$200/hr tiers.

Under the workload, the bathing and drying grooming steps were the most energy-consuming and hardest on my back. So, I came up with a new service: the "Full-body dry cut" option. This helped in many ways for all of us, like:

- Saving money for clients (cutting the grooming bill by 50 percent)
- Clients becoming masters of coat care at home (fewer mats on dogs between haircuts)
- Clients still getting a quality haircut by me.
- Puppies and shy dogs got the spa day split, so it was shorter and less tricky for them to deal with

- More manageable workload for me (95 percent were dry cuts only in the $200/hr tier, no bath and dry at the spa—clients did that at home)

I created a handout (pdf document) for my clients who chose this service that they got at the time of scheduling, and it worked out so well!

Outcome

When my client prospects heard the price difference between The Works (bath, dry, Face, feet, fanny, hairstyling by me) and the Full-body dry cut (hairstyling plus face, feet, fanny trim + them prepping the coat at home for me), they were more than happy to prepare their dogs for me, especially since they had my guidelines in the "Preparing the Coat for a Dry Cut" handout.

They knew what to look out for, and they did a fantastic job that I could easily work with. For short shaves, they had me do the trim first, and they did the bath and blow or air dry at home after the haircut. This was an unforeseen turn of outcomes for me, but boy, was it a pleasant one!

Food for Thought

Leave time to see the market changes and make sure you recognize and meet their needs. Add new services as needed!

Don't have time for 10–15 minute consultations about haircuts? Add a **Consultation service** and charge for it.

Want to help puppies getting used to grooming equipment but don't have time for it? Add a **Getting Used to Grooming Tools service** and charge for it!

Don't have time to deal with scheduling? Hire an admin if you want one and add a new **admin fee** so clients will cover the cost and it won't come out of your labor compensation.

Want to see the cost of supplies separately from the labor and fees? Add a **supply fee**!

Are you booked up but clients sometimes want to come before/after hours due to an urgent situation? (Other groomer canceled on them last minute before spay/neuter surgery, etc.) Offer an **Urgent Appointment service** and charge for it boldly. They will appreciate you working early/late and they can reimburse you for the extra exhaustion so it'll be worth it for both of you.

I see so many groomers curse their clients because they drop off/pick up their dogs late, or push for an earlier appointment. Regardless of how they present this to you, it can be an opportunity if you handle it like one. Someone wants to come today for a 60-minute trim? It'll bea $100 Skip the line! fee added to the grooming bill. Do they like it? Great, you can pocket a bonus for some overtime. They don't like it? Great. Now it's their call to say no, and you get to finish work on time.

Want to avoid bad reviews? Dedicate a ~15-minute **meet & greet** (one time fee) **for first timers** to talk about desired haircuts and possibilities with the current hair quality on the dog, and charge for it! Clients will feel cared for, and you can give clarity on the current coat situation and can talk about a desired haircut modification before doing any trimming if needed. You can schedule one right before the haircut or just as a first or second opinion on the coat as a standalone service. It works wonders and you get paid as if you were grooming at that time.

Clients need more education on coat care. They need resources, their dogs need training, and you need relief so you won't cry by the table due to pelted coats and a 10-blade shave all over the dog's body or because you got bitten by a feisty one. Offer it and charge for it! A **Coat care training service** can be where you discuss tools, how tos, dos and dont's, keeping dogs still, etc. It is great for heavy or tricky coats, like the kind doodles have, and clients usually have a bunch of questions about grooming anyway.

You can do it online, via handouts, or in person. This complements a short shave incredibly well, so you can let the client know you'll need to do a sporty trim today but it'll be the last one since they will have all the tools and tricks up their sleeve to avoid it in the future. You can have handouts printed or sent via pdf to clients about coat care between hair-cuts, how to find mats, how to resolve them, etc. I have a folder packed with almost sixty pages of handouts and a Spa Day Summary with a mat map for new clients. They are very happy about the gift and their skills improve so much after they study the materials at home. This helps them to get more info and refer back to it later, and it frees up my time, as I can explain less in words yet still give more information to clients.

Want to get some relief from bathing and drying? Offer a **Dry Cut service** for clients who are up for the coat preparation game. (It's not for everyone.) There are more people who can prepare the coat wonderfully than you think! I LOVE the dry cuts only without the need for hiring a bather. Have a handout for them about "Preparing the Coat for Dry Cuts" and you will be pleasantly surprised. Want my handouts? Get them from WholesomeGroomingAcademy.com!

Chapter 9

Results and Next Steps

My clients enjoy their freedom and autonomy to pick and choose services they need. I enjoy the time dedicated to specific services instead of rushing a talk without scheduling it. They get the service they need; I get paid for my time and can better serve my furry and human clients. Win-win-win.

My Revenue Almost Doubled in a Year

With my new rates set in place, I made $165k in 2021. From the previous year's $85k, it was a huge $80k raise for me that enabled us to buy an amazing house. I felt over the moon with the progress, and even my accountant shared how impressive of a raise I'd managed to get for myself in such a short period of time.

Quality and Value

As you can see, there is a lot behind why my services and quality of work are so popular. I wouldn't have succeeded if I just switched to $200/hr from $20/hr at the beginning.

I had to seriously train myself to meet the needs of a crowd above my own class. And it's hard, but it is very doable to accomplish with the right tools and mindset.

The Move

These new prices survived a move that we pulled off in a crazy real estate market in October 2021. We moved sixteen miles (20 minutes) away from the old location. About 10 percent of my old clients and 1 percent of my new clients chose to find a groomer closer to them. My services stood the test of moving very well. I was scared as hell, probably more scared than the raise from $10/hr to $20/hr, but the schedule was full 2–3 weeks in advance continuously, and 50 percent full about 1–1.5 months from there. So, though it was a big step, my clients were ready to pay and drive the extra 20 minutes for the quality and services I provided.

Next Steps for Me

I'm taking it easy with raising my rates now. This last one was a huge one, and I am spending time enjoying the fruits of the most recent sprint of getting the house we live in now with an ever thriving cash flow.

I feel fulfilled, comfortable, and respected. I want to enjoy life for now before finding another money block and going at it. It feels very nice to see that roughly 60–70 percent of all my appointments are dry cuts or FFFannies, so I get to skip bathing and drying dogs more often than not. This upgrade helps me a lot physically and it boosts my creativity.

The dedicated times for resting I squared out in my calendar inspire and energize me to publish my works that were dragging on for years, like courses and my book titled **Nail it!: A Step-by-Step Guide to Wholesome Dog Nail Trimming**, and to write new ones, like this book you are about to finish and the accompanying part 2.

Helping Groomers

I hear on forums left and right how exhausted, overworked, and under-paid groomers are. I've been there and got out of it. Helping groomers create a more fulfilling work-life balance for themselves is my next challenge I have taken upon. The best side effect of this is that dogs will enjoy the spa days under their care significantly more.

Knowing the difference between corporate workdays and workdays as a solo groomer with an exclusive practice fuels me to help other groomers get the relief and fulfilling life they need by yesterday. I want them—and YOU—to know how to do it step by step, and I want to help fine-tune your business so you can rejuvenate doggies in harmony with yourself, your doggy clients, and their owners.

Stay Tuned for Part 2

This book was all about the journey I took to get my business where it is today. I hope you found it inspiring. You can implement many of the strategies discussed as they are presented here to improve your work-life balance, or you can customize them to your liking.

In the second part of this book, I will focus on how can you reach your dreams way faster than I fulfilled mine. I will share how you can start and scale your own business today based on the lessons I've learned throughout these twelve years in the grooming field.

I will share all the nitty aspects about the business side of things—from website dos and don't, to setting up your business identity, to dealing with clients, to setting up your services and how much to charge, to wording your appointment confirmations, to getting your first client and seeing the signs of how to grow your business even further.

Whether you are a fresh groomer graduate or someone who is an employee but wants to break free and work in their own salon, you will learn all of the exact tools and strategies so you can start/switch with confidence and speed into this field.

Get the First Chapter of Part 2

Would you like to get the first chapter of part 2 of the book? Email me at betty@wholesomegroomingacademy.com with the subject line: "First Chapter Part 2" and I'll send it to you.

Pet Groomer App

The essences of what I've learned in customer care and running a high-profiting business are embedded in the grooming software Levi has developed for me and for other groomers: our **Pet Groomer App**[3].

His 30+ years in the software engineering field enabled him to create a software that is tailored to groomers' needs, based on my business profile (exclusive, solo-groomer setup), but it is flexible enough to customize it to meet the needs of other types of groomers as well, such as mobile groomers. We implemented loads of automations for customer care and business growth while keeping a friendly tone. The software is easy to use, loads fast thanks to an automatic server scaling that fires up more servers to meet demands in real life, and it runs reliably.

How the Pet Groomer App Software Came Around

Over the years, I've tried so many softwares and apps and they lacked critical features for my clients and me that resulted in time-consuming workarounds, giving up on the feature, or they had so many bugs weekly that I just couldn't bear it anymore, given I was paying close to $100 a month for their iffy service.

Levi was complaining that he didn't like his corporate work anymore, and I was complaining to Levi about the softwares I'd been using having issues constantly. He was getting tired of it, and I was getting tired of it. LOL.

---

3   http://www.PetGroomerApp.com

So, one day I told him, since you're listening to me while I'm pouring out why all these softwares suck, and I'm listening to you why you don't like your work anymore, why don't we jot down my thoughts in a positive form, like what does the app need to do so you could work for yourself and could create an app that really fits groomers' needs?

Funny enough, he connected with the mission of this app and got really excited about it. He decided to build the Pet Groomer App as his full-time job, getting out of the corporate world he dreaded so much by now as well. I am happy to announce that he is much happier working on the groomer software and has a way better work-life balance.

The doggy spa alone supported us both in the new house until we launched the app and it took off. The power of my methods can help support not only you but your family as well. In case your significant other wants to take a paternity/maternity leave or kickstart their own projects and needs a few months until it brings in revenue, your solo groomer business has the potential to support them.

You can learn more about the app here: www.PetGroomerApp.com

Courses for Groomers

I've created courses for wannabe, soon-to-be, or practicing groomers so they can create or convert their business to bring more fun and financial freedom for them in their everyday lives.

I have courses on grooming dogs by topics and on how to run your grooming business as well.

Check them out on my teaching website:

www.WholesomeGroomingAcademy.com!

Our Best Wishes to You

This is the little tale of my business's journey so far, in a nutshell, showing how I got to where I am today. I hope you enjoyed it! It was sure fun to look back and list the strategies we implemented along the way, and see how we overcame and learned from our mistakes.

We would feel honored if you'd let us in on this journey of yours and would love to hear and answer any questions you may have about starting/running your own grooming business! Feel free to reach out to us at any time.

You can reach me at my teaching email
betty@wholesomegroomingacademy.com
or by texting me at (512) 775-2471.

If you want Levi's help, you can reach him at levi@petgroomerapp.com. We'd love to hear from you and help you get where you want to be the fastest possible way!

We wish you good health and a wonderful journey in life.

Belly rubs to your dogs!

Betty & Levi

Suggestions for Further Reading

Here are the books I found incredibly helpful in pivoting my business over the years.

Marketing & Positioning

Obviously Awesome: How to Nail Product Positioning so Customers Get It, Buy It, Love It
April Dunford

Gap Selling: Getting the Customer to Yes: How Problem-Centric Selling Increases Sales by Changing Everything You Know About Relationships, Overcoming Objections, Closing and Price
Keenan

Get Rich, Lucky Bitch: Release Your Money Blocks and Live a First-Class Life
Denise Duffield-Thomas

The Lean Startup
Eric Ries

The 4-Hour Workweek: Escape 9–5, Live Anywhere, and Join the New Rich
Timothy Ferriss

High Performance Habits
Brendon Burchard

Communication and Mindset

Connecting Across Differences: Finding Common Ground with Anyone, Anywhere, Anytime

Jane Marantz Connor and Dian Killian

Say What You Mean: A Mindful Approach to Nonviolent Communication

Oren Jay Sofer

Nonviolent Communication

Marshall Rosenberg

How to Win Friends & Influence People

Dale Carnegie

Man's Search for Meaning

Viktor E. Frankl

Your Second Life Begins When You Realize You Only Have One

Raphaelle Giordano

Rich Dad Poor Dad: What The Rich Teach Their Kids About Money - That The Poor And Middle Class Do Not!

Robert T. Kiyosaki

Getting to Yes: Negotiating Agreement Without Giving In

Roger Fisher and William Ury

Dog Handling

Low Stress Handling Restraint and Behavior Modification of Dogs & Cats: Techniques for Developing Patients Who Love Their Visits
Sophia Yin

Grooming Without Stress: Safer, Quicker, Happier: Setting the 21st Century Grooming Table Up for Success by Employing Low-stress Handling Techniques
Terrie Hayward, Jay Andors, and Anne Francis

On Talking Terms with Dogs: Calming Signals
Turid Rugaas

Doggie Language: A Dog Lover's Guide to Understanding Your Best Friend
Lili Chin

Dog Grooming

NAIL IT!: A Step-by-Step Guide to Wholesome Dog Nail Trimming
Betty Peto

The Mutt Styling Guide
Chrissy Thompson

Theory Of 5
Melissa Verplank

Notes From The Grooming Table
Melissa Verplank

Health

Dr. Aviva Romm - AvivaRomm.com

The Institute for Functional Medicine - ifm.org

Please Leave a Review!

I would deeply appreciate it if you left a review of this book on Amazon.com. Your review could help groomers make a difference in their lives and their furry and less furry clients' lives, by growing their business further.

Check Out Betty's Other Book

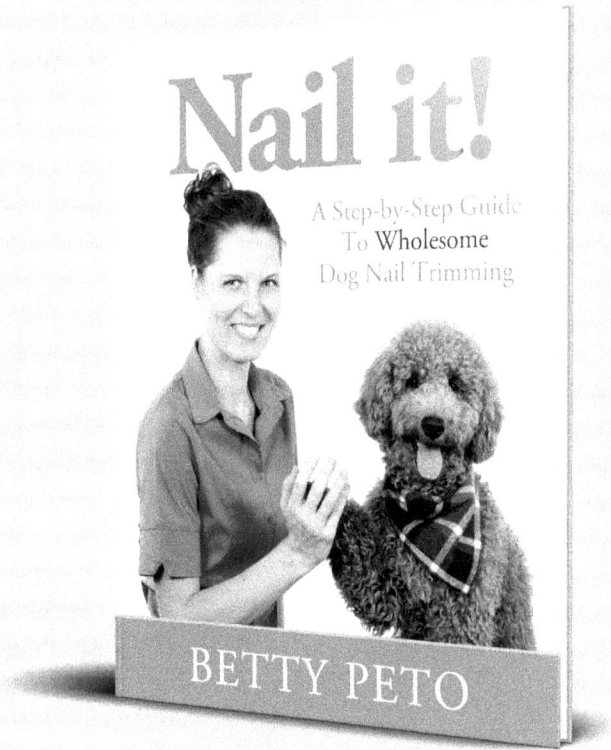

Nail it!

A Step-by-Step Guide
To **Wholesome**
Dog Nail Trimming

BETTY PETO

Available Wherever Books Are Sold

www.ingramcontent.com/pod-product-compliance
Lightning Source LLC
Chambersburg PA
CBHW051901090426
42811CB00003B/412